HOW TO BUILD GIANTS

13 Giant Steps Toward Authentic and Servant Leadership

Mikeal R. Morgan

This book is dedicated to my children:
Skyler, Brendin, Cameron, Trinity, and Mia.
It is by leading you that I first understood what servant leadership was.
After you, it was never about me.

HOW TO BUILD GIANTS

Cover designed by Mikeal R. Morgan

Edited by Ann Kellett – www.annkellett.net

Any resemblance to actual persons, living or dead; events; or locales is entirely coincidental, unless specifically called by name.

Mikeal R. Morgan
Visit my website at www.mikealmorgan.com

Printed in the United States of America

First Printing: November, 2019
Phoenix Training Innovations

ISBN- 9781691862696

CONTENTS

FOREWORD

by Jack Plating, former Executive Vice President & Chief Operating Officer, Verizon Wireless

ow to Build Giants is a terrific read. It incorporates time-tested principles with a strong emphasis on putting people first, along with practical strategies that are sure to strengthen any leader who implements them.

Mikeal's approach is authentic because of his more than two decades of experience successfully leading teams in multiple industries. He has done such a great job of incorporating the true leadership lessons, philosophies, and strategies that have helped shape him, as well as other leaders, along his journey.

Mikeal's passion to help others develop their own formula for success comes out in each chapter as he provides concrete examples and tips for each of us to consider in our daily work.

My hope is that you will not only read *How to Build Giants*, but will use these principles and techniques to lift your team to a higher level.

Giants are built when there is an intense, "all in" focus on people. The business and shareholders all win when leaders then leverage the giants they've built to take an "all in" approach to best align products, process, and people.

I encourage you to enjoy your time with this book. Really evaluate your own strengths and weaknesses as a leader. Your respective teams and companies will all benefit from your experience and the investment you've made.

INTRODUCTION

The world needs better leaders

"A genuine leader is not a searcher for consensus, but a molder of consensus."
—Martin Luther King, Jr.

The principle behind this book's title and this program's foundation comes from a quote by one of the most influential scientists of all time, Isaac Newton: *"If I have seen further, it is because I have stood on the shoulders of giants."* To me, that quote captures the true essence of servant leadership because if you are to see further as a leader, you must be able to stand on the shoulders of the giants you build.

I write in a straightforward manner that avoids five-dollar words and academic theories so that you can both understand and value the information offered. It will be up to you to implement what you have learned, so that you can build this program in your own way, with your own unique style. I hope you can appreciate the kind—but direct—approach I take to help people become the best leaders they can be.

THE GOAL OF THIS BOOK IS TO BE AS SIMPLE AND PROFOUND AS POSSIBLE, WHILE ALWAYS TELLING THE TRUTH.

Reading this book should push you to think and act differently.
Please keep an open mind and a humble heart as you read. While you are pushed to think and act differently, I will guide you through a simple, easy-to-implement outline of the program, an overarching strategy, and some practical tools that, if implemented correctly, could lead your team to success, regardless of industry. While the concepts are relatively simple, I have found that great progress comes from

successfully executing the often-overlooked basics of leadership. Simple blocking and tackling are often underrated strategies.

The research for this book came from the decades I've spent in leadership roles in both the technology and hospitality industries, deeply studying people, performance, culture, and team dynamics. I've coupled the things that I've learned on my journey with thousands of hours of interviewing and studying hundreds of other leaders to glean insight and wisdom from their more than five thousand combined years of experience—all here in this book for you.

IF NOTHING CHANGES, NOTHING CHANGES!

If you are a new or aspiring leader, read this book if you are willing to take the role of leadership seriously so that you may become something quite rare and wonderful: a *great leader*. Be willing to hear a wake-up call and to then take a hard and critical look at yourself and to put in the hard work required to follow the outline and personalize it so that it fits your unique personality and culture.

If you are already in a leadership role, be willing to engage in critical and real self-awareness. Don't brush off the things that you read in this book and assume that you do all of them perfectly; instead, ask yourself how you can take what you do to the next level. You may already be considered a great leader, and if so, then you understand exactly why you should read this book carefully, as every great leader craves development, new ideas, and new inspiration.

Leadership is one of the most challenging responsibilities on the planet, if done well. To think and consistently act as a great leader takes incredible discipline and balance, and a strong desire to fearlessly lead and serve others. Great leaders focus on people and are driven by the success of those they serve because they know that true leaders only win when those around them win, as well.

"If serving is beneath you, leadership is beyond you!" —Anonymous

We are in a new era of life and business that is very fast-paced and ever-changing; to become a great and continuously successful leader, you must be authentic and willing to *serve* others. It is only at this level that you begin to understand the paradox of obtaining success best described by the late, great Zig Ziglar: *"You can have anything you want in life if you are just willing to help other people get what they want."*

ONE HUNDRED PERCENT AUTHENTIC: BE THE LEADER YOU SHOULD BE, INSTEAD OF THE LEADER YOU THOUGHT YOU HAD TO BE.

Great leaders understand that perfect leadership doesn't exist. Great leaders know that they will fail many times and make plenty of mistakes on their leadership journey. And while failing isn't the goal, great leaders will tell you that they have always learned more from failing than they ever did from easy success. Because of this, great leaders are not risk averse, but instead are determined to learn from every failure. They also understand that the 80/20 rule *of leadership* means that people will point out what you do wrong eighty percent of the time while recognizing what you do right or well only twenty percent of the time.

Great leaders will never become leaders out of desire for fame, fortune, or power; in fact, great leaders know that to get power, you must *give* power! Great leaders know that they must inspire people to think, but not tell people what to think.

To quote William McKnight, the former CEO of 3M Company, *"If you put people in fences, you get sheep."*

And finally, great leaders understand that their job is to influence, not to interfere. *How to Build Giants* will show you how to incorporate these and other attributes into tangible actions that make a real difference.

THE GOAL IS AUTHENTIC AND SERVANT LEADERSHIP.
BUT WHAT IS THAT?

"I think being authentic and transparent is the most important aspect of leadership. If one understands his or her weaknesses and enlists others with the strengths that complement the mission, the team wins. The bottom line is to be honest with who you are as a leader." —Jack Plating

Authentic and servant leadership is described in many ways, but in general, they can best be described as being true to yourself, focused on the success of those you lead and not your own self-interest, while also being willing to make short-term and even personal sacrifices for the team's long-term gains. All actions taken by authentic leaders have their team in mind first. Being an authentic leader starts with being honest and real with yourself, hence the titles of the chapters in this program.

Authentic/servant leaders are rare. These traits, while easily discussed or written about, are very difficult to implement in today's fast-paced, high-pressure work environments. One of the main reasons these leaders are rare is pressure. Good leaders fundamentally understand good decision making and where their focus should be, but when the *pressure* of things like quotas or deadlines is applied or when things go poorly, many leaders revert to basic human emotion and simply *react*—and that is when the yelling starts. The end goal is to provide true, great leadership and an intelligent *structure* so that we get *more leading* and *less yelling*.

Authenticity is often elusive because of today's social pressures of political correctness and other garbage that keeps everyone thinking that the bullshit they see on social media and other outlets is the real world and what they should adhere to. And if you are simply looking not to offend anyone, take Steve Job's advice: "If you want to make everyone happy don't be a leader. Sell ice cream." Just don't mistake authenticity for being an asshole. In fact, I devote an entire chapter to pointing out that as a leader, you should not be an asshole.

"True leadership stems from individuality that is honestly and sometimes imperfectly expressed. . . . Leaders should strive for authenticity over perfection."
—Sheryl Sandberg

STRUCTURE IS IMPORTANT, BUT WHY?

Structure in life is important because it's what we know best. As humans, we've had a structure in our lives even before we were born. Before birth even takes place, we eat at a certain time, sleep at a certain time, and so on. When we are born, our parents implement structure as quickly as possible.

As we get older, our time, schedules, and days and nights become more structured because we eat at a certain time, take a bath at a certain time, and go to bed at a certain time. As we get older still, we gain additional structure with school, which prepares us for work, and so on. Even with no established structure, because we are such creatures of habit, we will find a way to impose structure.

The key is getting people to form good structure from good habits and to work within a structure that works for them, their clients, and company.

Without structure around your leadership, it is difficult to have consistent success. You may be thinking, but I have a plan and isn't that the same thing? No! In fact, to quote Mike Tyson, *"Everyone has a plan until they get punched in the mouth!"* Structure is different—it's bigger, better, and smarter than a plan. It is more wide-scale in that plans can and should live inside of a structure.

A STRUCTURE CAN HELP US SET PROPER EXPECTATIONS FOR OURSELVES AND OTHERS.

What are the right expectations for us as leaders or the teams we lead? I am a big believer that *good* people live up to the expectations put on them.

"The greatest danger for most of us is not that our aim is too high, and we miss it, but that it is too low, and we reach it." —Michelangelo

While I believe with all that I am that good people will rise to the expectations we put on them, you must start with good people. As Jim Rohn said, *"Don't send a duck to eagle school."*

How to Build Giants teaches to focus first on people. Authentic servant leaders must devote time, energy, and effort in hiring, caring for, and developing good people, and only then can we expect excellence from them.

Never be timid to expect excellence; just be sure you aren't expecting it from the wrong people.

ONCE YOU HAVE A BASELINE OF GREAT PEOPLE, YOU CAN USE A 'PROGRAM' TO CONDITION THEM FOR SUCCESS.

Conditioning is one of the most fascinating elements of development that I have come across in my decades of research and experience. In the animal kingdom, we have seen very interesting experiments that demonstrate how animals are conditioned. In one scenario, researchers placed a glass divider in the middle of an aquarium so that half the fish now lived on one side of the divider and half lived on the other. At first, the fish would bump into the divider and then swim off. After a while, however, they would swim right up to the wall and then swim away. A few months later, the divider was removed, but the fish continued to live only on the side that they were conditioned to live on when the divider was in place.

Had these fish simply tested the situation, they would have seen that the wall had been removed and that they had additional living space, more chances to find food, and so on. In our world, such a divider could be an old policy, and outdated procedure, or any of the status quo issues that exist out there. The question is, when was the last time that you or your team really "tested the walls?"

CONDITIONING, ALONG WITH PURPOSE AND OTHER KEY ATTRIBUTES, ENABLES THE HIGHEST HUMAN POTENTIAL.

One reason why leadership is such an awesome and difficult responsibility is because you deal with the human element. Human potential specifically is the most awesome and powerful thing on the planet, and as a leader, you have the great challenge of maximizing that potential! When we look at mechanical potential, there are definitive limits. An American, factory-built passenger car on a full tank of gas, for example, will go for X number of miles before it runs out of gas. Maybe a bit more, maybe a bit less, but within a small variance, we know when it will fail. It will go X MPH for X time with no oil in the engine compartment before the engine blows up, to give another example. The point is, there are defined and predictable limits with mechanical objects. But when we examine people, all bets are off.

There are plenty of stories of humans defying everything we know about human limitations. These include a hundred-and-twenty-pound woman lifting a full-size car to free her trapped child, or sailors stranded at sea for days without food and surviving longer than they "should have" based on history and what we know about human capacity.

Take speed, for instance. In the 1800s, people started measuring how fast humans could run a mile. By the early 1900s, it was deemed medically, scientifically, and humanly impossible for a human to run a mile in under four minutes. But on May 6, 1954, Roger Bannister ran a mile in 3:59.4.

Just seventeen days later, an Australian man by the name of John Landy also ran a sub-four-minute mile. By the end of 1957, more than a dozen people had done the same. These days, thousands of people have run a sub-four-minute mile, and in fact, there are boys in American high schools today who accomplish this feat regularly. We learn from people like Roger Bannister that most of the limitations we know as humans are self-imposed.

THE WORLD NEEDS BETTER LEADERS.

As cliché as that may sound, I believe it, and so should you. The world needs leaders who are willing to continuously invest in themselves and their teams and *do what is right, not what is popular* or *easy*. The world needs leaders who appreciate diversity and inclusion because they understand that what challenges us, changes us. And finally, the world needs leaders who care about people over process, and long-term, sustained success over a quick win at everyone's expense.

These are the leaders who understand that the only way for them to see further, longer, better, and more profitably is by standing on the shoulders of the giants they build!

In an often-thankless profession, I would personally like to thank you for taking this journey with me. Get ready to take some GIANT steps!

GUT CHECK 1: Keep an attentive mind and an open heart as you read this book. As a leader, you have an obligation to improve yourself and those you serve.

△ △ △

GIANT STEP ONE: MAYBE IT'S AN US PROBLEM

If you are looking for someone to blame, I know just the person to start with.

"You work for the team, not the other way around!"

—Gary Vaynerchuk

I hear it from leaders all the time: "My people just don't get it." Or, "My team just can't hit these targets," or "They don't pay attention" . . . and the list goes on. In most cases, leaders are quick to pass the blame before taking a hard look at themselves and what they are doing or not doing!

"If anything goes bad, I did it. If anything goes semi-good, we did it. If anything goes really good, then you did it. That's all it takes to get people to win football games for you." —Paul W. "Bear" Bryant

Coach Bryant was correct, and the same rule applies when coaching in business and in life. I am not saying to avoid coaching bad behavior or to not correct mistakes that people make; I am saying that we as leaders must take a hard look at the root cause and take the blame ourselves when our program fails the people we serve. Leadership is difficult in many ways and while others may be responsible for certain things, as leaders, we must be willing to accept the blame *first*.

Here is a great example of the blame game in the real world. As you read this, ask yourself if you are blaming others for something that you ultimately control.

I recently conducted a leadership development clinic for some mid-level managers. One of the participants said to me, "With all the technology in front of the teams during a team meeting, it's impossible to keep their attention. So, in my frustration, I physically removed their phones, tablets, and laptops during meetings." The first question I asked him was, "How do you now gauge their disengagement? I mean, if the meetings are boring, at least the technology gave you a gauge of distraction, whereas now their minds are still wandering and they're still not paying attention to the meeting, but you are unable to tell."

It is not a them *problem; it's an* us *problem!* We went on to discuss the content of his meetings, its relevance, and the way he presented it. What we uncovered was that he sat behind a table and too often presented material that lacked significance and in a manner that lacked conviction. His people's inattention wasn't to blame; the root cause was meetings that were ineffective, uninspiring, and lacked true purpose. And the issue is not entertaining a team or hosting a show instead of a meeting, either; it's about effective communication with people who respect their job, company, and leader—and all that starts with you.

We have an obligation as leaders to effectively communicate and to own the problems and concerns of our teams, regardless of where it seems the blame should lie. Stop the blame game and start believing that it is an US PROBLEM.

We see similar issues when it comes to meeting deadlines, hitting targets, and other responsibilities that must be fulfilled. Many times, teams try their best to meet all the expectations before them but lack the proper direction and planning to do so.

"I think self-awareness is probably the most important thing towards being a champion." —Billie Jean King

Running effective team and staff meetings is so important, but how do you address the blame game for the short and long term? **Self-awareness is the key!**

"Your vision will become clear only when you can look into your own heart. Who looks outside, dreams; who looks inside, awakes." —Carl Jung

Leaders who take the time to develop self-awareness are better equipped to fill the gaps in their own performance and their team's.

Many studies have proven how self-reflection and overall self-awareness can help a person become more humble, balanced, and goal oriented. The key is to believe the findings!

SELF-AWARENESS APPLICATION

As a leader, you should take ten to fifteen minutes each night to self-reflect. Find a place where you can be quiet and still, and ask yourself the tough questions.

Keep a journal of these things and work on them daily, or simply focus on improving one thing each day. It certainly doesn't have to be these specifically, but here are some that I use and that others have shared with me:

- What did I do today that was bigger, better, faster, and smarter than what I did yesterday?
- Whom did I learn from today?
- Did I ask for advice or help from anyone today?
- Whom did I listen to today?
- Whom did I help/serve today?
- Did I put people first? How?
- Did I communicate effectively today?
- Did I grow my network of people today?
- Did I positively influence/inspire people today?
- Did I simplify things today?
- Did I make good choices today?
- Did I make a mistake that I can learn from today?

If you answered no, nothing, or no one to any of these questions, ask yourself, how will anything change or improve tomorrow? Am I being honest enough with myself? Can I do more?

Finding the time to **be still** is a critical aspect of self-reflection. If you can't find a quiet place each night, try the shower. I do some of my best thinking in the shower.

If you can't seem to break away for quiet time at night, you still have control over this and can wake up earlier! Try four or five a.m.

"Five a.m. is the hour that legends are either going to bed or waking up!"
—Anonymous

Waking up early (before others) gives you time to be still and to think, plan, and work on administrative tasks before you get to focus on people. Most people instantly complain, telling me that they are not a morning person, that they can't wake up that early, and so on. These are all sad excuses. You have an alarm clock and the ability wake up early; the choice is yours. Great leaders are not lazy.

"People that hit the snooze button work for people that don't!" —Anonymous

GUT CHECK 2: Before you look to blame others, be very honest with yourself and first ask if there is anything that you could or should be doing differently! Are you setting the right example? Are you doing everything you said you'd do? Are you operating with urgency and integrity? Are you the first one in and the last to leave? If not, from whom should you truly expect more?

GIANT STEP TWO: DON'T BE AN ASSHOLE

No one respects an asshole

"Nearly all men can handle adversity, but if you want to test a man's character, give him power." —Abraham Lincoln

I f you had to apply for your own job today, would you get it? Would the reputation you have built even warrant an interview? Gone are the days when you could act any way you wanted and treat people any way you wanted, and it would be okay because you are the boss, or because you get results. It doesn't work that way anymore. *Sure,* you may be thinking, *I got news for you Mike— my boss is still a huge asshole!* Trust me—a shift is upon us.

They're called millennials (or Generation Y, born between the early 1980s and early 2000s). I am not convinced that they are as disloyal or lazy as they are often accused of being. I am convinced that they just aren't loyal to poor leaders like the Generation X and Baby Boomer generations are and were.

Think about it. We Gen Xers and Baby Boomers put up with assholes for years, hating life, and accepting whatever poor attitudes, yelling, and name calling they dished out. The millennial generation isn't like that. When so much talk about hiring and developing the millennial generation came out a few years ago, I read a quote that really stuck with me. It simply said,

"Millennials aren't disloyal; we simply demand better leadership."—Anonymous

That quote really moved me. It helped me look deeper inside myself to deliver better leadership. But let me be perfectly clear: I am not talking about being soft on people or not expecting people to work hard or do difficult things in their job. I am only talking about how we as leaders treat someone in our care.

I strive to be great to work for, not easy to work for.

Being great includes not being an asshole while still holding people accountable, and expecting them to work hard.

If you are already a "leader" and a real asshole, either change now or leave. Even if you get results, and have been in the role forever, "we" don't want you, and "we" don't need you. Don't be arrogant enough to think that someone who is kind and lifts others up can't get better results than you can by being an asshole. Leading through fear and tyranny is almost guaranteed to achieve two things: short-term results and disgruntled, disengaged employees. Instead, go dig ditches or something. Dirt doesn't take it personally when you yell at it or treat it poorly. Leadership is simply no place for you.

Being a genuinely nice person will give you an edge in leadership far more powerful than fear ever would. While we humans are unfortunately more motivated by what hurts or scares us than by what helps us, we must keep in mind that fear is temporary. Hold people accountable; just don't be an asshole while doing it. Respect and admiration are gained by serving others, can last a lifetime, and will give you the tools needed to build giants.

"If serving is beneath you, leadership is beyond you." —Anonymous

APPLICATION FOR BEING NICE

Literally focus on being nice, smiling, and caring for the people you lead as you would your own family. Get to know your direct team individually and understand what personally motivates each person. With a larger team, be collaborative when possible. Solicit ideas from the team on what might work *better*.

The five key things all people want and need to hear from a leader are:

1. *"What do you think we should do?"*
2. *"I'm sorry"*
3. *"I'm proud of you."*
4. *"Thank you."*
5. *"I believe in you."*

These five things, if said honestly and in a timely manner, will give your team an understanding of your admiration, respect, and appreciation of them. This is the cornerstone of good relationships and provides a stable and productive environment for open and honest dialogue. No one should feel above saying and *meaning* these things!

In the end, being an asshole is a choice; *you simply do not have to be an asshole.* You are the leader and have the power to hold those you care for responsible, up to and including terminating their employment, what do you gain by being an asshole? In fact, you can terminate someone and still keep their dignity intact without ever being an asshole.

GUT CHECK 3: You don't have to be an asshole to be effective. If you understand that fact but continue to be an asshole, please do everyone a favor and find a job that doesn't involve leading people.

△ △ △

GIANT STEP THREE: CLEAN UP THE MESS

Organization and Prioritization

"For every minute spent organizing, an hour is earned."
—Benjamin Franklin

I t will take you being very honest with yourself right now. Are you disorganized? Are you able to find things quickly, respond quickly, and have the resources you need readily accessible? People depend on you, so you can't afford to be disorganized. Being organized means that you can be more agile, faster to respond, better equipped to handle situations, and typically less stressed at work and home. Being organized with everything from your computer desktop and folders, email, desk and office area, vehicle, home, yourself, and more, matters! If you are disorganized, you will find it nearly impossible to *prioritize* because you will not have good visibility of all the issues that require your attention.

This is the downfall of many leaders. They are so caught up in their own messy web of disorganization that they lack time to spend coaching, communicating, and networking with their teams. So many leaders make excuses or tell you that, to them, the mess you see "is organized."

People use these excuses when one of three things occurs. One is that they are too lazy to get their affairs in order and take the time needed to clean and organize their life and keep it that way. Two, they lack the knowledge of what true organization is and how it can be obtained and maintained. Three, they refuse to delegate tasks so they could better handle the leadership aspects of the job. The latter of these is coachable and can be taught. But like anything, you should seek that knowledge and put it into practice. Read books on organization, talk to others about what they are doing to stay organized, and then—most importantly—stay with it!

Let me get tactical here for a bit and share my thoughts on organizing your email and other tools to keep you as productive and responsive as possible. I suggest starting with your phone, computer, and email. For your digital files, you should devise or adopt a filing method that allows you to quickly file and retrieve important documents. This way, you can keep your desktop and documents clean and organized, ready at a moment's notice. Organizing email is a bit tricky, and there are many platforms and ways that this could be achieved. I will share with you the filing system I use for email.

I have used this method in three different mainstream email platforms, and it has always worked well—so much so that my response time and ability to field and respond to emails is typically one of the first things that the new teams that I lead will notice. It is more than a methodology; it is a way of business life.

APPLICATION FOR EMAIL ORGANIZATION

1. Get your inbox clean by declaring *email bankruptcy*. Create a folder and name it with today's date. Move everything from your inbox to that folder so that you have a clean inbox. Most of that crap that you haven't answered yet has already been resolved and doesn't require your attention, anyway. You probably are hoarding other stuff because of some CYA fear instilled in you somewhere along the way. The point is, by creating this folder, you will still have all that old crap and can find something IF you really must, but you also are now able to start fresh with a clean slate.

2. Think of your inbox as a to-do list. As things come in, get them done, and after they get done, file them! Create a folder section that allows you to find things easily, if needed. I usually set mine up in three main folders with as many sub-folders under them as needed. The three main folders are People, Departments, and Team. People could be your boss, peers, others you deal with frequently, and so on. Departments are typically HR, Operations, and so on. The team folder is your direct reports, with a folder for each.

3. DELETE WHAT? The process for sending an email that requires follow up takes discipline. I delete my sent and my deleted emails. *What—why?* When I send an email that requires follow up, I BCC myself on it so that it comes into my inbox (to-do list). If a question comes back from the people I sent it to, or there is a need to loop others in, I delete all emails except the latest one. This way, I have the most current record of all the conversations; all other emails are incomplete and therefore, trash. Once this follow-up is complete, I file the final email in the appropriate folder. Most people keep every email they send, the responses, and so forth. The problem is that we feel as if we need to move fast and can't take the time to delete, file, and otherwise get organized. I submit to you that we don't have time not to!

4. Keep up with this methodology. Being organized is difficult at first and means being disciplined. The good news is that you can manage this even with your smartphone— there is no excuse not to keep up with it except a lack of discipline.

Now what? Use this newfound organization to your and your team's advantage. This goes back to "maybe it's an US problem." We can hold others accountable and coach to optimal performance IF the team has everything they need to be successful. This includes direction, information, response, approvals, etc. Never be the reason others can't do their job. So many teams lack clear direction and quick response time from their leader, resulting in a team member waiting around, being inefficient and ineffective because of their leader. With a clean inbox, you can respond faster and retrieve things easier, and thus be a better resource for your team.

Take a hard look at your smartphone and other digital tools, as well. I see far too many leaders literally scroll from screen to screen looking for applications and other tools. Instead, take thirty minutes and organize your applications by grouping those that belong together. This saves you minutes when obtaining data, allowing you to be even more responsive.

Don't stop organizing. You can further evaluate and work toward organizing other areas of your business, such as parts of the market that you own, offices, routes, deliveries, territories, products, services, and so forth. Take a good, hard look at how things could improve if properly organized. Are you getting all that you can from your available resources? Are other resources available that you are not properly using?

IF YOUR OFFICE AND DESK ARE CLUTTERED, YOUR CAR, HOME, AND MIND PROBABLY ARE, TOO.

Part of your job as a leader is to manage perceptions, and the first perceptions that others have relate to your appearance. The adage "you never get a second chance to make a first impression" is accurate. This includes your personal grooming, of course, but also the appearance of your desk, office, car, and other spaces. All these impact that first impression. To err is human, but the key is not to err on purpose. If you are disheveled, the probability that you are disorganized (and therefore not as responsive as you could be) is higher. In short, get your shit together.

DOING THE RIGHT THINGS DOESN'T MEAN MUCH IF YOU ARE DOING THEM OUT OF ORDER.

Now that you are more organized, you must be able to prioritize quickly and decisively. I see so many teams struggle, even when they do the right things, because they do the right things in the wrong order. So many salespeople prioritize administrative tasks over prospecting. So many leaders prioritize reporting and analytics over communicating with their people. There is a place and time for everything, and reporting and administrative tasks are included in that, but more and more companies are missing the forest for the trees when it comes to true priorities. Their leaders are blindly leading the charge or worse, follow the inefficient charge. As leaders, we must be able to discern which tasks take us closer to the end goal and which take us further from it. Time is the most limited and precious resource on earth and should be treated that way.

"If everything is a priority, nothing is a priority!" —Garr Reynolds

Do not make everything a priority and expect your teams to complete them all, the way you want them to. What will happen is that people will develop their own priorities and do things when they think it is best. For the record, that may work out better for you! But, if you have a method to the madness and need things done in priority order, then it is critical that you communicate as few true priorities as possible, so they are meaningful and important to all.

APPLICATION FOR PRIORITIZATION

1. Decide the priority of your goals. Do not take for granted that everyone knows exactly what this is; instead, write them out and then, as a team, collaborate and together come up with a series of tasks all of you can and will do (in your own way) to achieve these goals. Then discuss the deadlines, order, and priority of each.

2. Create a SIMPLE message around the goals and rank them in priority order. Make it something people can and will remember. People remember things in threes best. If your priorities are greater than three, you must consolidate and create a more strategic outline and only list three strategic goals and their priority. Just because you are in a complex business or hire complex people doesn't mean that all people inherently understand things that are complex. Your team will only accomplish goals they know and understand.

3. We do not think in words, but rather in stories and pictures. Most of the world's best presenters tell great stories and only use pictures as a visual aid to get points across to large audiences. To that end, create visuals, infographics, and/or one-pagers. People respond differently to different types of media, and often, a visual will help people interpret what you are saying better and faster. Don't take for granted that since people can read that they will understand what you write. Pictures, after all, are worth at least a thousand words. I cover this more extensively in the chapter on simplifying everything.

4. To maintain prioritization, ask yourself, and teach your team members to ask themselves, three important questions about every business activity you undertake:

i.   Is what I am about to do going to help me achieve my goals and get me results? If the answer is *no*, find a way to stick only to the activities, meetings, calls, and so on, that get you closer to your goals.

ii. Could this activity be done better, faster, or smarter? Could the agenda of this meeting be covered in an email instead? If so, why isn't it? Nothing changes if nothing changes. It starts with you!

iii. Finally, in what order should I tackle today's tasks? Make a list and number them in priority order of what best supports your goals, taking into consideration the deadlines for each.

If you can boil down the true priorities for your team, they will develop a keen focus and accomplish them more often than not. Keep priorities few, simple, and memorable.

GUT CHECK 4: Take organization and prioritization seriously. By being organized, you can be more responsive and effective. Take the time to get things organized and be diligent enough to keep them that way.

△ △ △

GIANT STEP FOUR: THE SECRET FORMULA

The Leadership Equation

Purpose will multiply both time and proficiency.

If two men are tasked with chopping a tree in half and the first man has only ever chopped one tree in half, but the second man has chopped a thousand trees in half, which will be better able to complete the task? The answer is both. The first man may only need more time.

Now imagine a third man tasked with chopping a tree in half. This time, imagine that not only has this person never chopped a tree in half, but also that he has limited time to do so. That's because a storm caused the tree to fall directly on his family as they drove into the driveway. The third man has an intense purpose for cutting the tree in half—to rescue his family trapped in the car. What are the odds of him completing the task?

Having a purpose—even if it is to avoid risk or a negative outcome—adds a multiplier to the equation that can literally change the game by intensifying both time and proficiency or negating them altogether. The third man, with no time and no proficiency, immediately grabbed a phone, called his neighbor and asked him to rush over with a chainsaw. He then called emergency services, and by the time emergency services got to the home, the man and his neighbor had freed the family and they were able to get medical care immediately.

The Secret Formula:

Time + Proficiency x Purpose = Game-Changing Results

The formula means that if someone or something has enough time but lacks proficiency and even a lot of purpose, they can still get results. Conversely, if a person has lots of experience and even a little purpose, and even if time isn't on their side, they can get results. If someone or something has time and proficiency, the addition of purpose multiplies the other two components, and the results are game changing. The formula has been proven in every industry, every sport, and every walk of life, regardless of the person's age, gender, or religion, and even holds true in nature and the animal kingdom.

WHAT HAPPENS WHEN YOU REDUCE PROFICIENCY? TIME X PURPOSE = ?

It has been proven that given enough time, one drop of water after another falling on a large rock, with the only purpose being gravity, will eventually pierce the rock.

WHAT HAPPENS WHEN YOU REDUCE TIME? PROFICIENCY X PURPOSE = ?

It also has been proven that water that is pressurized and blasted onto a rock with accuracy and skill will pierce the rock in significantly less time.

WHAT HAPPENS WHEN YOU REDUCE PURPOSE? TIME + PROFICIENCY = ?

I have taken on a number of things in my life, as I am sure you have. Usually, the first time we do that thing, we fumble around, do things wrong, out of order, and so on. BUT, if we have the time, we can still get it done. As we do more of it and become proficient, we need less time but still require some level of purpose, or these tasks usually get pushed aside.

Exercise and diet are fine examples. While people may want a "beach body," they usually only get serious when the *purpose* is apparent, such as a doctor telling them their health is at risk.

I was personally reminded of the purpose part of the formula each time I purchased a Christmas present for one of my kids when they were younger that stated "some assembly required." It is in these times that my purpose of putting together a complex toy that seems to have seventeen thousand pieces outweighs the time or proficiency aspects. The purpose for me building a toy for one of my kids and seeing their face on Christmas morning would literally give me the ability to find a way to become more proficient. I looked up how-to videos, or changed the game altogether and got help, delegated the activities, and so on. Where there is true purpose, the other factors of the formula become intensified. This is why the equation says the first two components are added, whereas they are both multiplied by purpose.

A friend remarked several months after I gave her this explanation that she had seen this concept play out many times in her life but had never been able to explain it in terms of an equation. She said that she had a recent epiphany when she traveled to my hometown of Houston, Texas, in the middle of summer and rented a car. She said it hit her, literally. She didn't think much about it when the airplane captain announced upon their arrival into my fair city that the temperature was a blistering 101 degrees with relative humidity sitting right around ninety-eight percent. She did, however, find out exactly what that meant as she opened the door of her rental car and the extremely humid heat washed over her in a wave that literally took her breath for a second. As she sat down in the driver's seat, sweating and panting, she realized she had never been inside that make or model car, and was almost amazed that it only took her a few seconds of pushing any and every button with a fan logo or a hint of blue in order to obtain some relief. She told me that although she had very little proficiency or time, cooling off became her driving purpose and allowed her to get the game-changing results she needed.

HOW DO YOU USE THE SECRET FORMULA TO BE A BETTER LEADER?

The secret formula will help you better prioritize and will serve two important purposes in the area of time management alone. It allows you to explain to your team how they should best spend their time, and it lets you know how you should spend your time with your team.

By using the formula as a filter, you can literally gauge how time is to be spent. if what your team members are doing isn't efficient, then they are taking away from the time component and will need to be very proficient to get results. This should push your team to check for inconsistencies in their time management, daily routines, meetings attended, emails sent, and so on.

If they lack skill, training, or proficiency, the formula should encourage them to think about getting the development they need in order to be successful. If they are skilled and experienced, and do fine with time, they will need to find and use their purpose to intensify their activities so that they can realize results.

Everything the team does should be passed through the filter of "is this a good use of time?" almost as a checkpoint of efficiency, proficiency, and purpose. In short, your team members should constantly ask themselves, "Do I have the skills and talent needed to perform this well? Why am I doing this? What is my purpose? And finally, how can I be as efficient as possible?"

As a leader, if you are not doing things to make your team or their work more efficient, or if you are adding unnecessary work, meetings, or even emails or other things that only confuse, distract, or delay your team such as lengthy or unneeded processes, then you are in effect taking from the time element of the equation and potentially hurting results.

If, as a leader, you are not adding skill, developing, training, coaching, etc., or reinforcing good habits and behaviors, then you are in fact taking from (or not adding to) the proficiency element of the equation.

And finally, we will talk in great detail about *purpose* in later chapters—how to discover it, channel it, and communicate it. Purpose, in my opinion, is the most critical element because with it, even if you lack the other two variables, you can still achieve results because purpose will multiply or intensify the other elements and allow for exponentially higher, faster, or better—even game-changing—results.

It is also important to focus your purpose and your team's purpose on positive things versus simply trying to avoid risk or harm. A sad and unfortunate fact is that humans are almost always wired to be more motivated to avoid what hurts us than go after what helps us, at least in the short-term.

In school, students are more motivated to study by the threat of failing out of school and losing a scholarship than they are by doing well enough to make the dean's list. In the workplace, employees will work harder or faster when their job is threatened for failing to meet a deadline or obtain a certain metric. While these are effective motivators for the very short term, if used indefinitely, the results typically have terrible, long-term repercussions.

While the example of a man chopping a tree to save his family worked well for that specific event, it would be difficult to maintain that amount of energy or stamina for a long time over multiple tasks.

Conversely, if a purpose is kept positive, we typically see where people can build on the momentum and actually improve stamina over time. Positive purpose takes a strategic approach and is where we see innovation, game-changing results, and even breakthroughs. There is a time and place for both "positive" and "negative" purpose for sure, and the key here is to form, and help the team to form, some type of positive, long-term purpose, regardless of circumstance. It is the difference in one person's purpose for temporarily avoiding a negative outcome (such as chopping a tree that has fallen on a car in order to save a few passengers) and transforming that into a positive, long-term purpose (to save many thousands of people by having automobile manufacturers build car roofs to higher standards).

We see this in many cases where the families of victims or survivors of tragedy or violent crimes—despite having a full-time job, no law degree, and no history of speaking to the United States Congress—are the impetus for changing laws or reforming some type of practice that improves everyone's lives!

Consider the secret formula in all that you do, and never underestimate the power of the intensification properties of purpose! I will use this formula throughout the *How to Build Giants* program to show why you should use it early and often, even when hiring.

Time + Proficiency x Purpose = Game-Changing Results

APPLICATION FOR THE SECRET FORMULA AS A LEADER

- **Evaluate the time aspect of everything the team is involved in.**
  - Is it as efficient as it could be?
  - Are you contributing to making things more efficient or are you taking from it?
  - When are meetings held?
  - Are too many meetings and calls being held?
  - Do the meetings add value, have strong objectives, or could this work be done via emails?
  - Do the current policies and procedures allow the team to move with speed and agility?

- **Evaluate the proficiency aspect of everything that the team is involved in.**
  - Does your team have the skills needed to perform at optimum levels?
  - Is there a development plan in place that allows the team to grow in skill level and proficiency?
  - Is there a mentorship program that could help your team build skills and proficiencies in new areas?

- **Help the team find and use purpose.**
  - Purpose is far and away the most important part of the formula, so focus heavily on helping people identify WHY they do what they do so that they can use purpose as a multiplier for everything they do.
  - Help shape purpose into positive, long-lasting fuel that will propel the efforts of the team.

GUT CHECK 5: Are you positively contributing, or are you interfering? Chances are, if you are not contributing to the team's time, proficiency, or purpose, you are potentially interfering with results. As a leader, you must first do no harm. Sometimes the secret formula lets us know that we should not insert ourselves at all into certain situations.

△ △ △

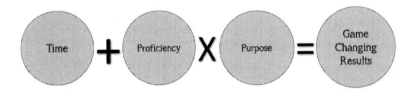

GIANT STEP FIVE: BUSY IS THE NEW DUMB

Busy is only busy, not productive

"Instead of saying 'I don't have time,' try saying 'it's not a priority,' and see how that feels." —Laura Vanderkam

A s I mentioned in the previous chapter, time is the most precious resource we have, and we must be sure that we make the most of it. Anyone in leadership must learn to master time management. We all have the same twenty-four hours in the day, so how are some people so much more successful than others? It all comes down to what we do with those twenty-four hours.

"Don't be fooled by the calendar. There are only as many days in the year as you make use of. One man gets only a week's value out of a year while another man gets a full year's value out of a week." *—Charles Richards*

How do you maximize your day and make the very most of your time? Your time as a leader should be spent on people first, simplifying anything and everything you touch, and inspiring everyone you come into to contact with, all while cultivating a culture of excellence.

Take the time to create strategies that win wars, and collaborate on better ways to win as a team. The only way that you will have time to do this is if you are as efficient and effective with time as possible and making the right choice about how to spend it. I used one of my favorite quotes from Laura Vanderkam in the subtitle of this chapter, but would like to share the entire quote:

> *"Instead of saying 'I don't have time' try saying 'it's not a priority,' and see how that feels. Often, that's a perfectly adequate explanation. I have time to iron my sheets, I just don't want to. But other things are harder. Try it: 'I'm not going to edit your résumé, sweetie, because it's not a priority.' 'I don't go to the doctor because my health is not a priority.'*
>
> *If these phrases don't sit well, that's the point. Changing our language reminds us that time is a choice. If we don't like how we're spending an hour, we can choose differently."*

I encourage you to choose and prioritize differently. As leaders, we can all easily get caught up in the busy, menial administrative bullshit that plagues every leader. It is up to you to take a stand to stop the madness and start using your time effectively!

Take stock in all that do with your time. Make a choice to change the things that do not make sense. Don't think that things like a standing meeting or task are good because they once served a purpose or made sense. They may not serve the same purpose—or any purpose at all—today. And even if you don't cancel certain meetings or tasks, you should still reconsider changing them if they aren't as effective as they could be. Reexamine every aspect of how you spend your time and ensure that it still makes sense!

APPLICATION FOR TIME MANAGEMENT

1. Check yourself! Be completely honest with yourself as you assess where your time is currently spent. Print off a blank page of a daily calendar that shows an hour-by-hour schedule, and start filling it out with what you actually did that day. This is one of the most impactful time management exercises you can do. Start at six a.m. and write down everything you did from six to six-thirty a.m., then move from six-thirty to seven, and so forth. If you wrote *sleeping*, I have already helped you gain an additional thirty to sixty minutes back in your day. Good sleep is critical for good health, but leaders don't sleep in. I will reiterate what I wrote in an earlier chapter about waking up early: People who hit the snooze button work for those that don't. You can literally knock out administrative tasks, work out, meditate, eat a healthy breakfast, read a book, or any other number of things to enrich your life in these thirty to sixty minutes that everyone else spends sleeping.

   Continue to work in thirty-minute increments through the day, documenting everything you did down to the slightest detail. This way, you can now take your goals and priority list that you created and match up to this list of how you spend your time and see if the things that you do contribute to your major goals and are in priority order. Adjust yourself accordingly. *Now, really do it. I mean, how many times are you going to hear and or read that advice before you do it? It took me reading it three times, hearing it four, and failing a dozen before I actually did this exercise well. It works if you do it!* Do this exercise with yourself before doing it with your team so you can share what you learned with them.

2. If it is important enough for you to spend time on, schedule it on your calendar. Whatever you use for a calendar should be your go-to for how you spend your work hours, so that you can make your own schedule while you are off. There are a few reasons for leaders to work extreme hours. Most are victims of poor time management. You should also not schedule every single minute of every day. If you only had $1,440, would you spend it foolishly? You have 1,440 minutes in every day, so spend them wisely. Again, time is the most precious thing on earth, so why would you squander it foolishly? Those who feel accomplished when they see a fully booked calendar are usually the same

people who mistake busy for productive. Ask yourself before scheduling anything if it is busywork or productive time before committing to it. Once you put it on the calendar, commit to it. The only thing I will caution here is that just because you blocked off an hour for a meeting or task, doesn't always mean that these things must take all of the allocated time. If they take less time, you should move on with something else and not meet for an hour because that is what the calendar said.

3. In fact, do not assign an allotted time to each task. There are many self-help/time management books and recommendations for assigning time to a task. I think that approach is dumb and here is why. I myself have been a victim of planning a productive task, scheduling it, and assigning a specific time and trying to stick to that time instead of perhaps looking for better and faster ways to get it done. You can literally condition yourself to take longer on something just because you have dedicated that amount of time for it. I found myself scheduling thirty minutes to plan my day and taking a full thirty minutes to do so. When I challenged myself and stopped assigning a time for the task, I did it in twelve to fifteen minutes. The only activity that you should expect to take every minute of the time allotted is a full body massage.

4. Limit social media and subscriptions. Ensure that the groups, people, and pages that you subscribe to are positive and uplifting. People, groups, or pages should be good things that add value to your life. I compare social media to legalized, socially acceptable, crack cocaine (only social media is harder to quit)! You can literally waste hours scrolling through feed after feed of multiple apps, watching someone else post selfies, check in to the gym, bitch about politics, or create a bullshit perception of themselves that couldn't be further from reality. Some social media can be okay, and even necessary depending on your industry; the key is to keep it in check and keep it positive. Some mobile phones offer a summary of the time you spend on your device, breaking down how much time and where you spent it, app by app. This can be very revealing and hard to accept when you see how many hours can be wasted in one day. Don't turn this feature off; instead, use it as motivation to use your time wisely.

5. For task-related activities, use your newly clean inbox as a to-do list and manage how you leave it at the end of the day. This way, you can email yourself additional things that must be done, if needed. Just be sure these to-do items advance your goals and are not just busywork! If they are bullshit administrative things, wait until late in the day or early in the morning to get them done.

6. Learn to say no. I love this quote from Michael Porter: "The essence of strategy is choosing what not to do." Sometimes we literally must have the courage to say no. Tasks that are just busywork and do not advance productive work should be eliminated, if possible.

7. Limit meetings that could be replaced with emails. Meetings can be a great way to communicate and come together as a team, but never meet just to meet. If there is nothing important to cover or nothing new to communicate, consider canceling the meeting or consolidating the meeting with another one. Bringing a team together just for team building and comradery can be immensely impactful if the meeting is designed for that purpose. This also goes for conference calls. Corporate America today will have calls to discuss other calls. I swear someone has some conference call quota somewhere and refuses to consider how damaging it is to productivity. What if every company had a director of meetings and calls and anyone wanting to schedule a meeting or call would literally have to "pass the worthiness test." What is the objective of the meeting? Who is it for? Could it be an email instead? What value will requiring people in a room hold? What value does this meeting hold? How will you make it engaging, and share the why behind the message? And so forth. Only if the person can answer these questions with confidence is the meeting granted and the invite sent. Since that will never happen, it's up to you to scrutinize the meetings you hold and even the ones you are invited to.

8. Avoid distractions at all cost. When you have meetings or one-on-ones with people, limit all distractions such as email and phone notifications. Check your surroundings and ensure that the place where you are working or meeting is

conducive to the task. Just as your time is precious, so is your team's, and as a servant leader, you must put their needs before yours.

9. Delegate. I know this one may sound obvious, but many leaders do not delegate effectivity. As an authentic and servant leader, you must learn to trust the people on your team. If you can't, you should fire them and hire ones you do trust.

10. Don't confuse *busy* for productive. Instead, provide clear, concise and *actionable* follow up for yourself and your team. After each interaction with your team and even your leadership; you should determine a few actionable items that should be worked on. This way everyone is on the same page regarding what work should and will take place and can be held accountable to productive, agreed upon work.

GUT CHECK 6: Are you busy or are you productive—and do you know the difference? Examine what you do and what you put the team through (meetings, emails, and other processes) and determine if these provide value or if they are just busywork. If they aren't adding value, stop doing them at once.

△ △ △

GIANT STEP SIX: DOUBLE DOWN ON CULTURE

Culture First – Strategy Second

"I used to believe that culture was 'soft,' and had little bearing on our bottom line. What I believe today is that our culture has everything to do with our bottom line, now and into the future." —Vern Dosch, author of Wired Differently

The questions isn't does your company and team have culture. The question is, is it any good? Is the culture an ever-evolving, inspiring one that moves people to win with passion and energy regardless of difficulties? Are you able to retain good talent even when things get tough? Building a great culture is the best investment a leader can make. Spend time starting, growing, and nurturing a great culture, as it will have an ROI that can't be matched. In fact, I recommend doubling down on culture! Before you invest in new systems, equipment, or training, double down on things that make a difference in your people's lives. This will challenge you as a leader, because most organizations see this effort as too "soft" or intangible to devote much time, energy, or resources to. It is your job as a leader to ensure that everyone knows how critical culture is within your organization. What is important to leadership becomes important to everyone.

The key is finding out what makes a great culture. What seems good to you or is perceived as good to others may not contribute to a great culture. Focusing too hard on the "cool factor" won't work, either. When stories of Google's work environment went public, other companies tried hard to mimic some of the perks in order to help build culture.

Google has dozens of free restaurants, free use of cars, on-site doctors that provide free checkups, wired workstations, laundry services, and on-site gyms. Shannon Deegan, Google's VP of HR, said in a recent presentation to his peers that, "This is not really the Google culture. This is the cost of doing business in our market." These things are the manifestation of what was important to those people.

Taking your dog to work won't work in every industry, but it does for Google. For example, I found the impressive thing that Google did as part of their culture was to encourage employees to spend twenty percent of their time each work week working on something they are passionate about. Through this, they get people to be even more creative and passionate about work! What does it cost them to do this? I would rather ask, what would it cost them *not* to?

IT DOESN'T COST MONEY TO DELIGHT PEOPLE!

I have witnessed leadership at several large U.S. companies that were desperate to build culture spend money without first finding out what is important. These companies only got to see rooms filled with ping-pong tables and espresso makers go unwanted and unused. I have never seen culture bought.

As an example, Netflix was one of the first, if not the first, U.S. publicly traded companies that completely did away with a traditional vacation policy. The company decided that it would not track how much time employees took off (an idea originated by an employee), but instead measure production and results from when employees actually did work. While employees can take as much time off as they want, they are still fully accountable for completing tasks and getting the agreed upon results of the position completed within the assigned timelines.

This option cost Netflix nothing, yet yields long-term, hard-working employees who passionately produce big results and have a vested interest in the company's success.

"Over the years we learned that if we asked people to rely on logic and common sense instead of on formal policies, most of the time we would get better results, and at lower cost." —Patty McCord, Chief Talent Officer, Netflix

THE POINT IS, CULTURE CAN'T JUST BE BOUGHT OR FORCED. CULTURE IS A SPIRIT AND A FEELING OF THE PEOPLE, NOT A THING YOU BUY OR DO.

The thing about culture is that it works like the parable that states that if you give a person a fish, they will eat for a day, but if you teach a person how to fish, they will eat for life. Similarly, when a company and a leader rely purely on strategy, rules, and policy to govern, they risk creating an uninspiring culture of compliance, fear, and zero-passion performance. This results in people waiting in a line for fish and focusing only on that day's meal. And they usually are pissed off about where the fish is served, how the fish is served, and the type of fish served.

People in this scenario get only the fish that you give. Even if your intentions are good, in this culture, people can truly only be as successful as you have dreamed. They are only as *nourished* as you allow. You have effectively limited the client experience, capped profit potential, and deterred the long-term tenure of great people, choking off the very life-blood of your company.

Conversely, if you create a culture of excellence, allowing people to have autonomy and a stake in what they create, they will passionately and relentlessly find new ways to win, forever! This point is eloquently expressed in a quote by Antoine de Saint-Exupéry, author of *The Little Prince*:

"If you want to build a ship, don't drum up the men to gather wood, divide the work, and give orders. Instead, teach them to yearn for the vast and endless sea."

In my early leadership roles, I struggled with the balance between good direction with the "why" behind it, and telling people exactly what to do. I felt that as a leader, it was always my job to provide this rather rigid "path" for my people to follow. I could see it so clearly: the goal was at the end of the path, and if they walked down the path I outlined, they would reach the goal. Simple and effective, right? Sure, if I were a shepherd and they were mere sheep. I learned that there are many problems when someone in a leadership role tries to be a manager. One is that I hired great people with tons of potential and then limited them to only what I was capable of thinking.

"It doesn't make sense to hire smart people and then tell them what to do; we hire smart people so they can tell us what to do."

—Steve Jobs

The second way this approach failed is that it fostered a culture of distrust. People felt as if I didn't trust them to get the job done effectively through their own initiative.

You may be thinking, *I can't just hire people and let them run wild!* You are right. A great culture is about hiring great people and then developing those people while fostering the right change, creating good and simple processes, and finally, trusting those people to follow and lead.

"If you put fences around people, you get sheep!"

—William L McKnight

I realized what a rigid structure I had when I participated in a one-on-one meeting with an employee and described the "path of success" I envisioned. As I explained how they could just walk down the path towards the goal, their brow furrowed into a look of puzzlement. The employee then asked the most profound thing possible: "But what if I can run? Or just fly over the path? Would that be okay, too?"

Here I was, literally limiting my team to walking, when many, if not all, of them could soar! There is nothing wrong with strategy, and standard operating procedures; in fact, I cover those in detail in the Simplify Everything chapter. Certain tactics within a strategy should be very detailed and structured but with an easy-to-follow standard operating procedure.

But policies must be balanced with free thinking. Culture thrives when people are sure of what they should do and are rated and measured simply and fairly. The important differentiator is that plans and operating procedures are more for developmental skills, administrative tasks, and other duties that require controllable efforts for consistent outcomes. On the other hand, a standard operating procedure should not be forced onto goals that require free thinking.

An example: if "delighting every client" is part of your culture's strategy, then writing a standard operating procedure around that is dumb. "Delighting" is a subjective term and its application should be left up to the great employees you hired.

It would be futile to try to formally define and describe every possible way of delighting clients.

If having a clean restroom is part of your plan to delight clients, then you can write a standard operating procedure tactic in support of that strategy regarding when, how, and how often the restrooms should be cleaned. The most important thing is to make having clean restrooms so much a part of the culture that your team takes so much pride in the job of cleaning the restrooms that they even come up with new ways to do so. This will keep your restrooms and your standard operating procedures relevant and fresh.

SO HOW THE HELL DO I LEAD MY PEOPLE IF I AM NOT SUPPOSED TO TELL THEM WHAT TO DO? THE DIFFERENCE BETWEEN MANAGEMENT AND LEADERSHIP!

"Slow down the macro (you got time) – Speed up the micro (get more done daily). This is what most have reversed." —Gary Vaynerchuk

What are the differences between management and leadership—and is one bad and one good? The simple answer is no, one isn't better than the other. In fact, to create the right impact and change in an organization and especially organizational culture, you must have both. Leaders are key in developing and communicating the overall vision and a strategy, whereas managers are responsible for the goals, tactics, and operational details in support of the vision. Both must hold their teams accountable for achieving results and operational excellence, honoring the company's mission, supporting your leadership program, and the rest of the team's responsibilities.

Leaders are responsible for taking risks, while most managers are encouraged to manage and mitigate risks. Leaders should be strategic, remaining more concerned and connected with people, relationships, and long-term impacts, whereas managers tend to stay tactical, focusing more on processes, problems, and short-term results.

Leaders should be careful to gather consistent input and give autonomy so that managers are not fenced in and become sheep! There is a delicate balance so that direction gets carried out, but with creativity and passion.

Leaders must adopt something I call **The Change, Not Results, Paradox.** This means being **results oriented, but change focused!** This simply means to quit focusing only on results or lack thereof. Instead, as a team, remain focused on changing and improving behaviors, habits, attitudes, processes, and skills, so that all of the people responsible for the results can better achieve them *in their own way!* The *strategy* is all about change and not about the result. After all, what if the target is too small? People in this culture can literally achieve more than the teams that came before them, because their growth isn't stifled and they aren't limited by a direction that doesn't fit them or was simply too constrained.

LEAD, NOT LAG, MEASUREMENT.

You can start achieving this by doing more "lead versus lag" measuring. Most companies today only do a good job of setting goals and objectives and then measuring results. There isn't enough being done to train, develop, and properly *measure* the human traits, skills, and behaviors that get these results. And then, when the reporting is completed and the goals are missed, the leaders are upset and seemingly shocked. Being very serious about and measuring factors like culture, behaviors, client satisfaction, and process improvements will help you head off poor results before they can happen. You are literally able to write the story as it happens and therefore write the ending you want!

Get feedback from the team on what actions, activities, and behavior-based qualities lead to great results, if not immediately, then in the long-term. And then bolster those things. Measure and hold a contest and celebrate when those things are done well. Great results always follow!

Old-style managers will say no to this idea because they feel as if they are already paying people to do their job and do not see this as being above and beyond that scope, or "celebration worthy." You must see past that, be different, and systematically implement behavior-based actions and tasks that lead to results.

PEOPLE WILL READ WHAT THEY WRITE.

Give choices when you can. In companies, as in life, there are outcomes that must be reached and goals that must be obtained. As a very young dad, I often grew frustrated with my daughter when she was about five or six years old and refused to take a bath. I spent a great deal of time and energy arguing with her—and sometimes even yelling at her. The end result was always the same. Both of us were frustrated and upset. I discussed the situation with my dad, who was first careful to clarify that yelling and screaming (being an asshole) was never the answer. He then asked me a simple, yet profound, question: "What is your end goal?" I said it was for my daughter to be clean. He suggested that the next night, instead of demanding that she get into the bathtub, to simply give her the choice of taking a bath or shower.

The next night, I gave my daughter this choice, and her little eyes lit up. She shouted, "All right—a shower it is!" At the end of the evening, my daughter was clean *and* happy because we weren't yelling or arguing about who was in control. She was clean *and* happy because I gave her the autonomy to decide, to have input into an otherwise strict outcome.

Before this, I was too caught up on a few things. One was me being right because I was in charge. Another was the quest for perfection. I was worried that she wouldn't clean herself appropriately or would get soap in her eyes, fall in the shower, or any other number of bad things. Back then, without experience and advice, I didn't see this as I now see most learning experiences, whether they are mine or someone else's. I now understand that they are usually messy as hell. They are stressful and sometimes go wrong the first or even the second time, and that's okay. As long as the situation isn't life or death, I have learned to be okay with messy lessons, and so should you.

Through the years, I have applied this in my leadership roles with great success. Sometimes, directions given by leadership must be strictly followed, but other times, if the end result is the same, why should we get hung up on the method? This is an example where there was not a "standard operating procedure" in place, only a goal of accomplishing cleanliness and happiness, and therefore, giving autonomy worked really well. I will tell you more about when to challenge the status quo later, but remember this:

"The seven most expensive words in business are:

We have always done it that way."

Building a great culture takes hard work and means getting people to think and act like leaders. This means that you as a leader will need to relinquish power in many cases.

TO GET POWER, YOU MUST GIVE POWER! TO GIVE POWER, YOU MUST TRUST YOURSELF, YOUR PROGRAM, AND YOUR TEAM!

The bad news is, one of the hardest things for most leaders to do is to give up control and power. Retired U.S. Navy Captain David Marquet wrote a book called *Turn the Ship Around: A True Story of Turning Followers into Leaders*. In it, he does a fantastic job of explaining how he accomplished getting his team to think and act like leaders. He explains how, as a submarine captain, he encouraged leadership from everyone and gave autonomy without pause for nearly everything that happened on the vessel. He vowed never to give another order, except one: the launch of a weapon such as a missile or torpedo. He did so because he said that launching a weapon would result in loss of human life and he didn't want that on anyone else's conscience—that this was his moral and ethical responsibility alone. I love David's message and highly recommend his book.

When you give power, you are actually getting something! You get everyone to think like a leader and make better decisions, allowing your business to become more agile, with strong, decisive leaders who care about the result without you ever having to mention it. This is dangerous only if you haven't developed them properly first.

Take the time required to study and practice this. When you *trust*, develop, and encourage your people to think like leaders, they will become invested in the company and the future. Through building a culture based on trust and transparency, your business becomes powerful and profitable, long-term.

In his book *What Would Google Do?* Jeff Jarvis wrote:

"There is an inverse relationship between control and trust. Trust is a two-way exchange, more than most people (especially leaders in power) realize. Trust is a mutual relationship of transparency and sharing—the more ways you find to reveal yourself and

listen to others, the more you build trust. Give people control and we will use it. Don't, and you will lose us."

AN EXAMPLE OF GIVING POWER: THE INVENTION OF THE POTATO CAPTAIN! TURNING EMPLOYEES INTO "INTREPRENEURS."

Great cultures have team members who have a sense of ownership and pride in what they do. So it's up to you to give them the autonomy to do so. While leading a team at a pizza restaurant in my twenties, I often consulted with a friend who ran a buffet-style restaurant in another town. I had experience in the kitchen and could solve most of the back-of-the-house challenges, but needed help in the front of the house to smoothly ensure that the various areas of the restaurant were maintained, cleaned, stocked, and so on. This was a particular challenge because my front-of-the-house staff mainly comprised teenagers or part-time, "non-career-minded" types. My friend told me that I needed Potato Captains!

My friend's restaurant served higher-end food, including steak, which cost them more money. One of their goals was to push baked potatoes, because they were filling and cheap, and therefore saved on food costs and increased profitability. My friend had a problem keeping enough potatoes baked so that he didn't run out (they take about an hour to bake) but also didn't have too many that they would grow cold and lose quality. His other concern was maintaining a fully stocked, clean potato bar. They say that necessity is the mother of invention, and my friend needed to reinvent the potato game!

He had a printing company create a fancy name badge that had room for a name under a gold-embossed title of "Potato Captain." The next day, he approached one of his employees who did a good job of cleaning and sweeping and seemed committed, but perhaps needed a little purpose in his job. He approached this young man with a proposal for something important, something that had never been tried and that could re-shape how the company made money.

He presented the young man with the opportunity to be the first-ever Potato Captain! The first thing my friend did was discuss the gaps in supply and demand with the potatoes and what it cost the restaurant in hard numbers. He also explained that this impacted the image of the restaurant's overall cleanliness and other ratings.

The Potato Captain, therefore, had a great responsibility, indeed! It would be up to the Potato Captain to manage all things related to the potato bar. He would now be fully responsible for keeping the right number of potatoes in stock, baked, and ready. He had to maintain a clean, stocked, and presentable area that would be appealing to customers and that would sell more potatoes. My friend even offered to pay the Potato Captain a small return based on the performance of potato sales.

With great pride, the young man accepted the position, and his sense of pride was instantly apparent. He kept a close eye on the stock levels, size, and quality of the potatoes. He kept the area meticulously clean and maintained. He polled customers to see what other toppings they wanted on his potato bar and made suggestions to management for other low-cost topping options. Within six months, the Potato Captain had made potatoes the most popular item in the restaurant, increasing potato sales by forty-three percent and decreasing food costs by a whopping sixteen percent. The increase in potato costs paled in comparison to the benefit of the overall decrease in food costs and with that, the potato crisis was averted, food costs were lower, profits were up, and the Potato Captain was praised, rewarded, and felt a sense of real value and purpose.

What my friend had accomplished was transforming a regular employee into something some have termed an "***intrepreneur.***" This is a person who thinks like an entrepreneur inside a company. I immediately stole the idea and turned my own restaurant team into a bunch of captains! I saw immediate improvements in every area, including restroom cleanliness. As each captain took great pride in their area, they began taking more pride in everything in every area.

They developed a leadership perspective and an owner's mentality. The sense of ownership and pride also significantly reduced turnover. Business owners rarely abandon their businesses, and when your team members feel like business owners, they stay! We were able to keep the exact same staff in place for two years, and in restaurants, that is almost unheard-of.

Tenured staff will stay motivated to save your company a ton of money and help drive the value of your brand. Conversely, staff turnover can be very costly and hurt your brand. I have successfully implemented the Potato Captain idea in every industry I've worked in, and at every level.

BUILD THE CASTLE OF GLASS, WHERE TRANSPARENCY IS CRITICAL.

You will read several times in this book about how transparency builds trust. More than that, in a culture where people can anticipate change, movement, and growth, they can be instrumental in helping steer the culture in the right direction. In my experience, even when change is negative, transparency helps people deal with loss and motivates them to do the right thing by the company and the client because they knew what was coming. A business that operates under shrouds of secrecy and on a need-to-know basis will have employees who spend more time gossiping, spreading rumors, and feeding misinformation to others than on working to achieve company goals! Worse, your people will not be invested in the business.

Be transparent with more than just top-line financials and targets. People will be more invested in something they help to build and will do all they can to grow a business that they are a part of. If people aren't involved in change, they can't possibly help implement it, and in fact, in most cases will hurt the process by speculating and spreading rumors and misinformation. Leaders should demonstrate how the team's efforts tie to the end result of impending change, and how critical their buy-in is to its success. With this approach, even non-management personnel will buy in and get behind goals because they understand how they can impact the result.

When I ran a pizza buffet restaurant in my early twenties, I explained our food costs to my cook and other kitchen team members so that, for example, they understood that for every four times they didn't scrape all of the pizza sauce out of the container, and threw away the container and the residual sauce, we could have sauced one more pizza. And while that seems like a tiny thing, these tiny things add up, especially when you empty nearly thirty sauce containers each day. I was careful to hire only people who cared and wanted to know how even a single behavior cost us money as a company, and how they could help make positive changes. I took the time to further educate and explain that when we could save money because of good habits, we could afford to invest in new equipment, upgrades to the restaurant, additional staff, marketing, salary increases, and the overall long-term success of *their* livelihood. The result was cooks who thought as kitchen managers, working with a sense of ownership and pride.

HOW TO BUILD GIANTS

WHAT YOU CELEBRATE WILL GROW! THE MAGIC PEN AWARD.

Recognition and celebration of even small victories are critical for building and sustaining a culture of excellence. Some leaders are reluctant to celebrate too often, believing this would turn their culture into a participation medal environment, but I am here to tell you that you must foster a culture where behaviors and small victories are also celebrated and rewarded appropriately. Maintaining the spirit of being results oriented, but also change focused, means you must be prepared to celebrate the behaviors and attitudes that lead to the desired results, and then celebrate those results differently when they are accomplished. In case you haven't figured it out, recognition is hard work. It takes time and energy.

But these are the things leaders do, because these things build long-term success in your team environment. Take the time to devise a smart recognition program that rewards certain behaviors. Schedule time to create the plan and revise it regularly so it stays relevant and up to date. Ensure that the recognition program is not only relevant and leads to results, but also that you communicate it effectively and incentivize it appropriately, as well. I have personally been in a situation on more than one occasion where I won a contest or was being celebrated for some accomplishment that I didn't even know I was in the running for, so it meant very little to me. If the milestones are not measured and communicated, you are not maximizing the recognition program.

One time, I took over a team as a new manager in a restaurant, and my leadership told me that I should be driving sales in the restaurant by getting the team to up-sell. They told me the task would be difficult because all the contests they had run in the past fell flat, with little to no buy-in by the team. I asked what they used as an incentive and was told that the budget was $25. After speaking with the team and getting an understanding of what was important to them, I announced a contest. The team member who upsold the most would win . . . *the magic pen!*

I explained that this seemingly cheap, ordinary ballpoint pen possessed the ability to mark one entire, four-hour work shift off the calendar so that the winner could take off and still get paid! The team could barely contain their excitement. Because I took the time to find out what the team enjoyed and wanted, not only did we upsell more than any other team in the restaurant's entire history, we also saved four dollars in prize money doing it. At the time, the team members made $5.25 per hour, valuing a four-hour shift at a grand total of $21. So, the incentive was not about how much money was given but *how* the money was given. It is critical to have good and creative recognition programs and to incentivize correctly. The magic pen can work in your organization, too, if you find out what people care about and use that to incentivize them.

WHATEVER YOU TOLERATE WILL ALSO GROW.

You will need to do certain things to protect your culture. As you communicate what attitudes drive excellence, you will need to also communicate that poor attitudes that destroy culture will not be tolerated, such as spreading rumors, gossiping, naysaying, dishonesty, lying, or being purposely offensive. These things will destroy your culture and must be addressed quickly.

HIRE CULTURE WARRIORS—FIRE CULTURE KILLERS!

A team is much like a human body in a way and can suffer from its own cancer-like behaviors. Cancer pops up, is dangerous, spreads rapidly in most cases and, while tedious and potentially dangerous to remove, if left alone, will further harm or even kill the body. Culture killers act in a similar way and therefore must be similarly removed.

When hiring, most leaders look for candidates who are highly skilled, but they also must focus on how well a candidate would fit into the organizational culture and then hire the most skilled of those candidates. People are remarkable and can be trained if they have the aptitude; but like cancer, people can seldom change who they are at their core. In fact, you will need to make some difficult (or not so difficult) decisions when it comes to who on a team you take over stays and who goes and do the tough job of cutting out the proverbial cancer.

In most cases, you will find people on a team who should not be there—and the ability to get results is not all I am talking about! I will use a sales team example here. If you run a team of ten salespeople and the top person kills culture but produces twenty percent more than anyone else, that person is usually seen as the one who can be an asshole, but this is ignored because they are producing. The truth is, that person is a liability, not an asset.

Here's why. If that person is a true culture killer, then the twenty percent more that they produce pales in comparison to how much more the collective team could accomplish if they worked in a great culture. There is actually a quick return on investment for firing culture killers, so get rid of culture killers quickly. This will not be popular in results-based environments, but you must ask yourself, are you in it for the short term or the long term? *Leadership isn't about doing what's easy . . . it's about doing what's right!*

Culture killers are harmful in any industry and can turn into workplace bullies because of what they are allowed to get away with. Their behavior is ignored because of their technical proficiency or other desired expertise. Some years back, I worked with restaurant owners as a "cleaner" of sorts. I was paid to observe what was going on and recommend changes that would result in higher profitability and market share. My responsibilities weren't limited to marketing or menu prices, but also included staffing, hiring processes, training and development, and more. One day I was contacted by a restaurant owner who felt she had some issues regarding declining sales, food quality, customer experience, and staffing.

I agreed to help, and part of my process was a three-day observation of her establishment. I observed what could only be described as a toxic employee who was single-handedly bringing down her place of business. The young man in question was a top performer in terms of technical skill and experience, and had a hand in many of the functions around the restaurant. He also had a terrible attitude, and was rude and disrespectful to all the employees and even to some of the customers.

When I asked the owner about the young man, she stated that he was a top performer and that he covered as many shifts as needed, never complained to her about anything and could work in any capacity they need him to work in, so she considered him valuable. When I explained his terrible attitude toward staff and customers alike, she didn't seem shocked. She said that she felt as if his availability and technical ability outweighed his poor attitude. I also let her know that I spoke to others on her staff to get their opinions on how he impacted them, the customers, and the restaurant overall. When I shared their personal accounts with her, and went over what we believed this man cost her in terms of staff retention and repeat business, she *was* shocked.

I let her know that this young man's reputation had preceded him to the extent that customers told the other staff that no matter how good the food was, they would not eat there if that meant having to see him. The staff even remarked that they had trouble recruiting and retaining good talent because no one wanted to be subjected to his mean comments and rude behavior.

In short, what my client had was a culture killer who was costing her more business than he brought in. With her permission, we terminated his employment the next morning.

Almost instantly, a feeling of relief swept through the restaurant. The entire place had new energy. Everyone stepped up to assist everyone else and the shift ran better than it had in months. Soon, productivity was at an all-time high. People were energized and didn't mind the slightly additional workload because they weren't being treated poorly. Just a few months after hiring a replacement with half the technical experience but a great attitude, the needle moved even further in the right direction.

Inside the restaurant, we painted two walls, tweaked the menu slightly, and wrote a training and operations manual. Outside, we re-landscaped the entry and adjusted the hours of operation, but did very little in terms of marketing. We wanted to see the effect that firing a culture killer had on sales before we took additional measures for marketing.

Word was out, and the employees recruited the best staff in town to work with them. Customers talked, too, and in the first sixty days after the firing, the manager received more than a hundred comments (verbal or on comment cards) about the "positive energy" and "delightful atmosphere," or the "great food and great service." Staff and customers alike responded to the new sense of pride and positivity created by removing one person—and sales showed it, too. Four months after firing the culture killer, sales had increased by sixteen percent. In one year's time, sales increased by twenty-nine percent.

Don't be fooled into thinking that your business or office is not suffering if you have a culture killer. To what extent is hard to say; this is very dependent on your industry, size of your environment, and number of culture killers. Please never think that one culture killer can't be the reason for poor sales, productivity, high employee or client churn, etc. But in case you do, I will close this topic with the words of the Dalai Lama, who said, "If you think you are too small to make a difference, try sleeping in the same room with a mosquito."

CREATE A COMMON ENEMY!

"People like to love, but love to hate!"—Mikeal R. Morgan

In any environment, peace and love should be encouraged, but there also is a place for "good hate." Think about it like sports fans for a minute. Most sports fans like, or even love, one team more than all others and therefore support the team, cheer for them, etc. BUT, when "their" team plays its archrival, the intensity of this cheering and support (and even ticket sales) grows! I suggest zeroing in on one of your top competitors and building some friendly fun around "good hate."

In one sales office I worked in, the sales director dressed a stuffed monkey in a one-piece baby outfit and wrote our competitor's name on it in sharpie.

He proudly announced that if you lost a deal to the competition, you had to come over and kiss the monkey's hand, and if you won a deal against them, you got to take out a little aggression by kicking the monkey around a bit! It was harmless fun that people gravitated around. The sales director also staged piñatas in the shape of our competitor's logo in the various offices and during meetings, we took them outside and beat the heck out of them. People loved having some fun with a competitive spirit around a common enemy.

Even if something like this has never been done in your office or work environment, and even if it's met with some opposition, press the matter and see how it works for your teams. You should have seen the faces on the senior partners of a law firm client of mine when I suggested this to them in their stuffy law office. They apprehensively agreed and it is now one of the highlights in every one of their offices.

Don't forget that no matter what industry you are in, it is the people who make up the culture and people like what they like, even if it isn't your preference. After all, this is a program for servant leadership. You must make up your mind: Do you want things that are only your preference, or do you want a top-performing team with a winning culture where people stay and produce results? *Nothing changes if nothing changes.*

YOU SET THE TONE, BUT IN THE END, CULTURE IS EVERYONE'S JOB.

You must consider culture the *most* important thing so that it becomes precious to everyone else. You set the tone and others will follow. Be careful to communicate how important culture is and the purposeful things you are doing to drive it. Ask the team what they are doing to create a great culture, as it is a team sport and everyone's responsibility! You will gain consensus from the team on what is important to them and their role in it. This way, there is mutual accountability in protecting the culture!

CELEBRATE THE SMALL STUFF AND GIVE POSITIVITY A SOUND!

Sometimes we can't be afraid to make a little noise. In 2008, I led a team of experienced, talented, highly skilled individuals with the worst attitudes I had ever seen! Every day, team members would come in, toss down their bag, and mumble some (un)pleasantries like, "Another day in paradise," under their breath before begrudgingly getting to work. I would ask for any good news, something that we could celebrate individually or as a team, and every day I got more of the same blank stares and mumbling.

I knew I needed to overhaul the toxic environment—and quickly—but in a way that allowed them to own the experience. I explained that sharing good news is a great way to be happy about the great things happening in our business each day but that aren't typically shared or verbalized, even if these were small, seemingly unimportant things. I knew that if we could start sharing some good things that were happening around the office, we could show people that there were things to smile about!

I encouraged sharing small victories like not getting hung up on, or getting to work with only minimal traffic, or enjoying a good cup of coffee, and so forth. The team was encouraged but still reluctant to verbally express these trivial wins, so I decided to go about it a different—and slightly louder—way. I purchased a small, silver call bell for each team member and simply asked each person to ring the bell to acknowledge anything they perceived as good news, with no explanation necessary.

The buy-in was as expected. A few folks almost immediately bought in and rang the bell once or twice a day for various things, and a few refused to even remove the bell from its plastic packaging. With each passing day, the bells rang more frequently and by more people because psychologically, people want to belong and participate. As the trend of bell ringing continued and grew, even the most reluctant team members finally joined in to ring their bell!

This was followed by a new trend. When one person rang their bell, others also rang theirs as a show of support. In addition, people began verbally sharing the great news that caused them to ring the bell. Attitudes began to improve, the culture began to shift, and almost instantly, we created an environment of positivity in which people not only looked for a reason to celebrate, but shared it with others so that everyone became energized. This all began with a prompt to look for and share anything positive; the bell merely opened a door for people to express the good happening around them. The sale teams coined the term "WIMB" for "where is my bell" when they heard something great but didn't have their bell.

The highlight of this transformation was when the president of our division emerged from her office and asked what all the bell ringing was about. When we explained that she was hearing the sound of good news and positivity, she smiled and said it was music to her ears! It didn't hurt that productivity by way of sales surged by over twenty-six percent in the quarter after the bells were implemented.

The next quarter, we continued ringing our call bells for the small stuff and also took things to the next level by installing a forty-two-inch gong in every office for big news! Unless you work in a library, don't worry about a little noise and disruption for the right reason!

In times where ringing bells and gongs isn't appropriate, find another way to share even the smallest success with your team and the sound of positivity will be the voices of proud, successful team members lifting up one another.

YOUR CULTURE IS UNDER ATTACK EVERY DAY!

You should think of culture as a game of offense and defense. Offensively, you are communicating, being transparent, giving power and autonomy, hiring culture warriors, etc. But you must also always stay on the defense. Defensively, you must monitor culture for defects and anomalies, and sudden breaches. Some of the things that disrupt culture are rumors (squish them quickly), the competition (get ahead of it and create your response), poor leadership (a.k.a. assholes—get rid of them), culture-killing individuals (get rid of them), and confusion (provide clarity). In addition, there are all kinds of bad changes, and you'll need to get ahead of them and reiterate the benefits of the job, company, and so on. Creating and sustaining organizational culture is hard work, so stay on the defensive.

Damaging rhetoric, poor attitudes, and negativity are extremely contagious and spread fast.

Never forget: "People like to love, but love to hate."

IF YOU CALL SOMEONE A KING, OTHERS WILL TREAT THEM LIKE A KING.

When I worked in the hospitality industry, part of our culture involved providing an *experience* for people, not simply a meal. We were pushed and incented not just to impress, but to "wow" people through a memorable experience for every guest who came through our doors.

We were also not allowed to call them customers—they were valued *guests* and should be known and treated as such. Sometimes, subtle changes in vernacular alone help people get more of a sense of value for people. For instance, in the technology industry, I encourage the team to refer to clients as clients, not customers. Nothing wrong with customers, but customers are transactions-based consumers that buy muffins from a bakery; on my team, we have clients instead. We are experts, and other experts (like attorneys) have clients because clients are valuable, long-term participants in their business lives. I have also seen companies that refer to the client as "the boss," calling them only ma'am, sir, or Ms. or Mr. Last Name. By truly considering customers as their boss, the team members innately became more subservient and attentive.

Internally, too, what you call people matters. I call the team I work with, a team. Not staff, not employee, not worker, but the team. The definition of a team is "two or more people working together," and that is what we live every day.

LEADERSHIP MATTERS IF YOU CARE ABOUT LONG-TERM RESULTS!

You may have heard that people don't quit their company—they quit their boss. I'm not sure I totally agree. I think people quit bad cultures, and leadership is a huge part of that. Leadership can literally make or break companies, and will certainly make or break culture. I have conducted hundreds of interviews in my research, and more than eighty percent of the people I have surveyed said that they had left at least one job that had good pay and good work conditions or a bright future, because of a bad relationship with their direct leader.

Conversely, nearly ninety percent of those I surveyed said that they stayed at companies that had a long commute, lower pay, and/or less-than-desirable office conditions all because of the culture, specifically naming the influence of a great leader they worked with.

In business, if you want to drum up some quick revenue, you reduce your price. If you want to get profits in the right direction, you balance your books and reduce expenses. But if you really want a long-term, sustainable, and profitable business, double down on culture. Hire the right leaders and let them lead and stay focused on what matters most—your people!

YES, YOU SHOULD STILL "PRAISE IN PUBLIC AND CRITICIZE IN PRIVATE."

Years ago, legendary coach Vince Lombardi was quoted as saying, "Praise in public and criticize in private." Today, there is an emerging trend that says this approach is wrong because it undermines your leadership or your team, or has other negative impacts. Please do not buy into that. In a team environment, make no mistake that people will understand who is and who isn't pulling their weight. If that person or group simply can't do the job, you should replace them, but publicly calling them out just isn't right.

I have believed that praising in public and criticizing in private was the right thing to do my entire life, but like many, I have seen the opposite of this play out in unfortunate ways right in front of me, many times. The weirdest and perhaps funniest example of this was when I was a frontline sales rep in the late 1990s. I worked for a major technology company that had scheduled a large meeting to discuss with employees the significant change it was undergoing. The director at the time announced that anyone who was not on time for the meeting would be dismissed, immediately and permanently!

On the day of the meeting, all one-hundred-plus employees showed up at the office about an hour prior to the meeting. Well, almost everyone, but with such a large group, no one could really tell who was and wasn't there. The meeting began and about twenty minutes later, the door swings open and in walks one of our teammates! As she makes her way to an open seat, our faces went blank and jaws dropped as we stared at her and then at the director, whose face was already turning blood red. He stops the meeting, looks at this woman and says, "What in the hell are you doing? I told everyone that if you were late, not to bother showing up! There is no excuse! How dare you!" The lady looks up, smiling slightly as she blushed and with a firm voice said, "I was going to be on time but on my way here, I shit my pants and had to go home to shower and change." Completely shocked and probably somewhat disgusted, the director finished turning completely red and went back to presenting the materials he had prepared for the meeting. Publicly confronting people without all of the facts is simply risking too much, typically at the employee's expense.

Another, more serious and sad time that I was able to witness this good and practical advice not being followed was when I was a kitchen manager in the '90s. In an all-hands meeting with the kitchen and wait staff, the general manager began talking about service levels and how it was everyone's job to be better at serving customers, and how we all played a role in one way or another. He then decided to single out one of our more tenured servers and let her know that he had noticed that she was not keeping up as well as the others, and that she needed to "get it together."

The young lady's eyes welled up with tears, and she broke down, sobbing. As we all looked on, she began to tell the room about how her husband was killed tragically in an auto accident two months prior, leaving her to care for her two young children alone and with little money and absolutely no help. She described how she was now working multiple jobs to pay the already-behind mortgage before she and her children became homeless.

Needless to say, the general manager apologized, and we all came together to help her and her children, but the damage had been done. He hurt an already emotionally broken woman in public for no reason! Had he simply asked her in private what was going on, she could have explained, and then we could have helped her and not only avoided a very nasty and embarrassing scene, but he would have also had a much more loyal and dedicated employee. This is one of the ways that leaders build loyalty and a brand that stands for putting people's interests first.

It is in no one's best interest to publicly call out that one person or group for not meeting expectations. In fact, doing so is detrimental to the culture and morale of the entire organization or group. Even if only a small group witnesses this behavior, word of publicly embarrassing actions spreads like a virus throughout an entire organization.

That person or group of people should be talked to privately and asked questions to uncover what is really going on. After all, we are leading people, and people are complex and have things going on outside of work that will impact what they do and how they do it. If after a private discussion it is determined that there is a legitimate gap in performance that could be addressed, the appropriate action should then be taken to improve the behaviors, habits, attitudes, and skills that are causing the poor performance. You can—and will—destroy culture by publicly ridiculing people, especially when you do not completely understand what's behind the situation.

MAKE SURE THAT PRAISE IS LEGIT BEFORE STATING IT PUBLICLY!

The practice of publicly recognizing people—while important—can backfire if not done with care and good information.

During my research interviews, I was told a story about an unfortunate situation that happened in an employee meeting in which over one hundred people had gathered to hear updates about the company and to see senior leadership recognize worthy people for various achievements. In the meeting, a staff member received a distinguished award for work he had not personally done. Over half of the people there knew this, and they reacted with shock and disbelief.

The woman who had actually done the work sadly shook her head before walking out of the room, no longer able to control her emotions.

This avoidable event, the result of misinformation passed to the senior leaders, stung the culture with weeks of banter, rumor, and gossip regarding unfair treatment and favoritism.

The flawed process turned good intentions into a bad situation, and created a stigma that had to be overcome.

PAY PEOPLE WHAT THEY ARE WORTH.

A peak performance culture where you get great results will come at the cost of paying people fairly. Pay is considered fair when your top performers can earn the same pay within about a ten percent variance at a similar job elsewhere. Paying people fairly is not only the right thing to do; it means that you can rely more on things like meaningful work, leadership, work/life balance and other factors to grow the culture and your business. Even if you don't set the pay initially for your team, you should evaluate the pay of each person who reports to you and ensure that it is fair.

The first thing I do after taking on a new team is to evaluate each person's compensation. I would sit down and carefully examine each person's pay and if it was not what it should have been, investigate why this was the case. If I determined it wasn't where it should be, I petitioned HR to change it. I was successful every time because I had done the research and prepared a business case for each situation. When I presented my team member an equity increase, I gained immediate credibility and trust with that person. The fact that I put them and their pay first meant the world to them. If you run a sales organization and only fifty-five percent of your salespeople consistently make quota, chances are you don't have a bunch of shitty salespeople— you have quotas that are too high. You only save money in the short term, and the cost of replacing great salespeople will far outweigh these savings.

PAY GREAT LEADERS WELL, TOO, BECAUSE YOU CAN'T AFFORD POOR LEADERSHIP!

According to research conducted by the Blanchard Group a few years back, the average organization loses an amount equal to seven percent of their annual sales because of poor leadership practices. That analysis found a fourteen-point customer satisfaction gap, a sixteen-point employee productivity gap, and a forty-five-point employee retention gap that translated into more than one million dollars for the average organization.

The bottom line is that poor leadership is costly in one way or another, and it's not always a glaring number on the P&L. In fact, it could be way more money than researchers could quantify! In other words, in my opinion the cost of poor leadership on culture, and the long-term impacts of losing quality people or not being able to attract top talent, is immeasurable.

WORK AND PLAY TOGETHER. TEAM-BUILDERS ARE WORTH EVERY DIME!

Show me a culture where people consistently get to know one another outside the office and I'll show you an office that can build personal bonds with teammates, understand and work better with one another, and get more done collectively than an office that doesn't gather outside of the office. I am not talking about "forced comradery," but people work with people and are inherently social creatures. People will work *well* with people they like and trust. Sponsor or get a sponsor for team-builders, company picnics or the like for your office, even if you are on a budget. Even if you work for a company that is a supplier or vendor, you may be able to use vendors or supplies of your own to help pay for an outing. Keep in mind that it is the kinship, commonalities, stories, and happenings that come from outside the office that often help build the culture within an office. This doesn't have to be an all-the-time thing, but should be part of your culture.

IF YOU AREN'T GROWING, YOU'RE DYING.

Much like plants or animals, people will stay and grow where they are thriving. Development is a critical part of the culture for that reason. Ensure that you have solid development plans in place for teams at every level of your organization and that you make development readily available and a part of the culture. Development achievements should be publicly recognized and promoted. Activities such as shadow days where you can effectively cross-train individuals not only increase your workforce's knowledge, but also help employees value the work of other departments and facilitates purposeful movement within your organization. People want to know that they have options, and if you don't provide them options internally, they will naturally seek them elsewhere.

PAY ATTENTION TO EVERYTHING.

"We listen to the whispers so we never have to hear the screams."
—Native American Proverb

Years ago, I adopted an old, Native American proverb into my leadership practices: *"We listen to the whispers so we never have to hear the screams."*

In English, *silent* and *listen* have the same letters, and I'd like to think that is for a reason. As leaders, we must check our egos and shouldn't believe that we must always know every single thing that is going on in our team, but we must be willing to find out what's going on in case action on our part is required. The good news is that you don't have to have some super, all-knowing power, or even have to guess what this might be.

As leaders, we must sometimes be still and quiet, and listen intently, paying great attention to what is being said, even if it isn't being said loudly. We must pay attention to body language and other nonverbal cues of the people we serve. We have to be careful because often these are little, seemingly insignificant things that we may want to chalk off to petty gripes or whining.

While it's true that you can't please everyone, even one or two people complaining about something is very different than whispers and may become a trend, joke, or grumble spread by multiple people through the entire office or organization. The latter can become dangerous and damaging to culture, and you should pay a great deal of attention to them, regardless of their size or current priority, and then take care of them swiftly.

Never think that you or your organization is too big to worry about small things. My favorite Benjamin Franklin quote is, *"Beware of little expenses. A small leak will sink a great ship."* Lastly, be sure you act on whispers quickly and then do something that creates positive change.

CULTURE TAKES TIME.

"People don't want to embrace culture shifts because it's not going to happen in the next twenty minutes." —Gary Vaynerchuk

Establishing a culture can take time, and in some cases it requires more time than most leaders are willing to invest. You must endure the hard parts and continue the behaviors that will lead to great cultures. One of my favorite expressions that I hear employees in a poor culture say is, "The beatings will continue until morale improves." You can change that. You can change the course of your company, but you must first believe that you can, and then make the investment in culture. This starts with your team and your department, but if you create a great culture, it can and will spread.

One of the best culture-based leaders I have ever worked for is a man named Jason Smith. Jason taught me the power of employee engagement and how a dynamic and magnetic company culture rich with enthusiasm and fun could propel an entire organization to new heights.

Jason was able to create a true movement that people fought to join and stay a part of. Once the movement was in place, the work became more fun than work, yet we achieved results that had never been achieved before, all while reducing turnover and improving the client experience. Jason also showed me that it took time, effort, energy, and a healthy dose of humility to build a strong culture.

I remember having serious, often lengthy, meetings to plan things like '80s-themed rallies or summer cookouts. We were always humbled at Christmas, when Jason dressed as Santa and had his direct team dress like elves (green spandex tights and all) to do a complete, choreographed dance for the larger teams.

Jason was also famous for putting his leadership team in positions to serve, in order to build culture. These were activities such as serving the community or contests where leaders washed a team member's car.

Even though it took time, energy, and effort, and the results were not immediate, Jason persevered and prioritized culture, proving that investing in culture pays dividends in every measurable result.

"Culture is a never-ending process." —Denny Strigl

APPLICATION FOR CREATING A CULTURE OF EXCELLENCE

- Understand that culture is not something you can buy or give, but a feeling and spirit that lead team members to believe in the company's purpose.
- Hire responsible people you can trust, then trust them.
- Find out what is important and good for your people, your business, and the environment that you work in and then foster simple gestures that make it easy for these things to happen frequently.
- Give people clear direction and hold them professionally accountable, but don't micromanage. To do so is unproductive and insulting.
- Focus on establishing an environment where you regularly encourage candor, transparency, and trust through good and honest communication.
- Give power and autonomy. Don't focus on having followers; focus on creating leaders—leaders who think and act as you would, or better!
- Listen, pay attention, and allow people to openly voice their opinions and thoughts, and then be silent for as long as it takes to thoroughly understand what they say.
- Make professional development part of your culture. Make it available, expect it, and praise developmental achievements.
- It should not only be okay to have fun—it should be encouraged. As leaders, we are in the people business.
- Dedicate time, energy, and resources to developing a great culture.
- Be patient when building a great culture and know that it takes time, and that it is never-ending.

GUT CHECK 7: *Enhancing and improving your team's culture is the most important work you can do as a leader. People make the difference. Where there is a culture of excellence, people will find innovative ways to be successful. That said, how much time are you devoting to making a positive impact on your team's culture?*

△ △ △

GIANT STEP SEVEN: LEAD WITH PURPOSE

Others will follow when they believe how you believe.

"We are drawn to leaders and organizations that are good at communicating what they believe. Their ability to make us feel like we belong, to make us feel special, safe and not alone is part of what gives them the ability to inspire us." —Simon Sinek

What is your *purpose*, your belief, your . . . *why*? *Why* do you do what you do? What do you *believe*? If you haven't identified these things, you may be underserving your team or yourself. Many leaders fall into one of the following categories: either they don't really know or can't articulate their purpose, or are too scared to put their purpose out there for everyone to see. *Those who truly lead with purpose are different, rare, and special.* These are the leaders who know and can articulate their purpose. These leaders can also effectively communicate their purpose, but most importantly, these top one percent *live and lead* with purpose.

PURPOSE MAKES IT ALL MAKE SENSE.

"After all, a quarter million, quarter-inch drill bits were sold in the United States last year and no one needed a quarter-inch drill bit—they needed a quarter-inch hole." - Leo McGivena

For most things in this world, people are not looking for what a thing is, they are looking for what the thing *does*. When it comes to purpose, whether it's people, companies, or products, people are looking for a *why* behind the *what*. Does your team work on something that they can believe in, that inspires them, and that connects them to something bigger? And what can you do to foster this? People want and need purpose and to have meaningful work.

Leaders who are truly in tune with their purpose are not merely leaders; these are the people that truly inspire as they lead.

I reference Simon Sinek quite a bit on this subject as I feel he is the foremost expert on the subject of purpose, which he calls "The Why." In his book *Start with the Why*, Simon writes, *"Leading is not the same as being the leader. Being the leader means you hold the highest rank, either by earning it, good fortune or navigating internal politics. Leading, however, means that others willingly follow you—not because they have to, not because they are paid to, but because they want to."*

I believe in Simon Sinek's research and thoughts about identifying and starting with why. Simon's articulation of what he calls *"The Golden Circle"* and why successful leaders and companies always start with not the what or how they do what they do, but rather the *why* they do what they do. This is the simplest clarification of something that I have believed in for so long but could never quite articulate like he does. Simon talks a great deal about how *"people don't buy what you sell, they buy why you sell it."* And this means not just buying in the traditional sense of a commercial transaction, but buying as in the buying of ideas, thoughts, and mindshare.

Not only are people more likely to follow you if they believe what you believe, but they are almost always also more productive and happier, take better care of your clients, and stay with the company longer than if they do not. When you are surrounded by people who believe how you believe, you are more likely to inspire them. This differs from motivation because inspiration moves people at a deeper level, and if you have the right people and the right *purpose*, your people will be self-motivated through the short-term *because* they have a purpose.

In *Start with the Why,* Simon goes into great detail and gives powerful examples of how leaders like the Wright brothers, Steve Jobs, and Dr. Martin Luther King, Jr., were so successful because they started with why they did what they did. These great leaders and innovators changed the world because people followed them for what they believed.

It wasn't until I finally heard Simon Sinek explain the concepts of The Golden Circle that I knew it was what and how I believed, and how I had seen success as a leader. I also know now that I follow and admire Simon Sinek not because of what he says, but *why* he says it. I believe this way because I have personally seen it work for years. To better understand and benefit from this principle, please read Simon Sinek's book, *Start with the Why.*

TELL PEOPLE YOUR PURPOSE AND YOU CAN HELP THEM FIND THEIRS. RALLY THE TROOPS!

In 2009, I ran an outside sales team for the largest telecommunications company in America. Every day, my team and I shared energy at an eight a.m. rally. These were not meetings or trainings; we had those too, but these were different and separate from any of that. In each rally (while it may sound strange to some), I enthusiastically shared with the team stories centered around my convictions and beliefs. And then as a team, we all shared a variety of stories of why we chose to work for the company and what our work meant to us personally, on a deep and emotional level. As deep and emotional as these were, don't get the wrong idea—these were high-energy, inspirational rallies, not quiet support groups! But we weren't just trading energy and stories; we were inspiring one another. When other leaders saw these rallies, they would come up to me afterward and ask how I found the energy or even enough stuff to talk about in order to rally every morning. For me, it wasn't something I had to even prepare for. It was meaningful, fun, and high energy because my team and I believed in our purpose, so talking about that purpose was easy and natural!

For me, working in telecommunications, I *believed* in my heart and was passionate about "improving the world by improving how we connected people." Our *purpose* was to connect humans to other humans (the *why*) and we just happened to do that through reliable, simple technology (the *what* or *how*). We had an obligation to one another and to society to ensure that people were well connected.

As a leader, I believed that we had the best team in any industry and what we did each day mattered. I believed that we had the ability to change lives and business in a big and meaningful way! I believed that if my team won, I won. My purpose as a leader was not centered on me or my success, but to grow my team members to become as strong, smart, and resilient as possible. *In short, I wanted to build giants!*

What I did by sharing these convictions and getting the team to share theirs was certainly motivating and got the energy flowing, and while this served some short-term goals for motivating the troops, they also were a catalyst to get us to discover and communicate *our purpose*. I have seen leaders who have great influence and such a positive impact on their teams with this practice, but who do not see consistent results from their influence. In these situations, it may not be your inability to influence, but that you may just need to increase the frequency of your influence. Like everything, there must be balance, so learn what the right amount of rallying, meetings, and other activities of direct influence are and then push yourself to execute with passion and conviction.

CHRIS FINDS HIS PURPOSE.

"People don't buy what you sell, they buy why you sell it."
—*Simon Sinek*

I had been unknowingly leading with purpose for some time and knew the principle worked, even though I couldn't clearly articulate the process. It wasn't until I personally witnessed how leading with purpose not only saved an employee, but also connected him to new levels of success, that I started putting all the pieces together.

In late 2009, my leadership approached me with some proposed personnel changes, including moving a young man named Chris to my team. At the time, Chris was highly stressed and significantly underperforming. What they didn't tell me was that Chris's underwhelming performance had landed him in the final stages of a plan that significantly limited his career with us. Chris would be seeking new employment unless he turned his production around, and quickly.

I approached his current manager and was told a colorful tale of my soon-to-be new team member.

"Good luck," she said smugly. "Chris is a bit of a loose cannon with a bad attitude." She described how he frequently got upset and how seemingly small things angered him. She also said he didn't take direction well and had outright refused to do many of the required, sales-generating activities. Candidly speaking, to say that I was not exactly thrilled to get someone with this reputation on my team was an understatement, but I had learned to put only limited weight on what others said, and to carefully form my own opinions.

I will never forget the day I finally met Chris. He was a big man, standing six-foot-three, and built like a professional athlete. Within the first few minutes of conversation, I learned a few things about Chris. He had a big smile, was incredibly intelligent, and had played some professional baseball until a shoulder injury ended his career. He shared with me his passion for creativity and inventing products that helped people. He also shared his successful track record of sales, so I knew that he had the technical ability. He had the skill, but lacked the will.

He told me how he had been successful in sales for several years at another company, and had only been with our company a little while and hadn't seen the success he was used to. He went on to say that during his short tenure with our company, he loved the work and the company, but that he and his manager never quite got along. I asked him to explain what he meant, and he went on to say that she only barked orders and yelled at him. When I asked how that made him feel, he said something very profound: "She is a micro-manager. She only cares about numbers and seems to have no purpose. She doesn't seem to believe in anything bigger than herself, and that is not very inspiring."

I knew from that moment that Chris wanted to believe in something and someone. In short, Chris wanted to be led.

While Chris was skeptical and I am sure a bit uneasy about the short time he had to turn things around, I felt right away that he would mesh very well with my team and how we did business.

The entire team embraced Chris immediately. For the first several weeks, we talked a lot about *teamwork* and what that really meant. We rallied and shared stories as a team about why we worked here and what was important to us, or our purpose. We lived out what it meant to be a true team and supported one another and remained focused on behaviors and attitudes rather than immediate results. We wanted Chris to feel not just welcomed but like he belonged and had a sense of purpose. I didn't know it at the time, but what we really wanted was for Chris to find *his purpose*.

Within a short time, Chris had a noticeable change in energy, attitude, and overall presence. His demeanor was much calmer and he had a sense of genuine happiness and peace when you spoke to him.

Chris focused on changing not only his results, but he told me that he also wanted to change people's poor perception of him. He was concerned that he was thought of as a short-timer with a bad attitude. I assured Chris that he could indeed change people's perceptions by consistently doing the rights things and having the right attitude.

Within a month, Chris surprised the entire office with his renewed attitude and desire to succeed. The man who was once withdrawn and subdued, reluctant to speak during our morning rallies, now led them with unbridled passion and enthusiasm. He produced more sales-generating activity than the rest of the team—combined. I coached him, keeping him focused and true, but he did the heavy lifting, and with a great attitude. We ran sales calls together and he did a good job, followed up, and had some decent traction. We continued to rally, support, and care for one another as a team.

Within two months of joining our team, Chris's sales results turned around in a big way. Suddenly, he was closing deals right and left and leading the team in sales results. During the third month, I rode with Chris on a sales call—one that would turn out to be very different than the other ones I had gone on with him.

We sat in the client's office and Chris beamed with enthusiasm. He almost instantly launched into explaining in detail how we rally as a team each morning and how we share why we work here and what it means for him to work in telecommunications. Chris said that he loved what he did in telecommunications because he connected people by connecting *with* people. He went on to discuss how the team had each other's backs and how we supported one another's clients if the need arose, because that is how we would want to be treated ourselves. Chris continued, talking about how excited he was to get to work each day so he could connect even more great people to one another!

Just when I thought he was about to go into why we were there and start probing into the client's business problems and determine how we can help, he didn't. Not only did he continue talking about the team and the culture that we created, but he also recited our team's positive affirmation chant that we said at the conclusion of our morning rallies.

At this point, I was almost beside myself, thinking, *this client is about to freak out and ask us why we are wasting his time.* Just when I was ready to kick Chris under the table, the almost overly attentive client caught my eye. He quietly leaned forward, literally on the edge of his seat as he listened intently to Chris so eloquently describe nothing more than *why* he did what he did and with whom he did it.

And then something beautiful happened—the something that Chris had experienced for the last several weeks as his sales skyrocketed. Chris went silent and the client leaned even further toward us and spoke these words: "I don't have any clue what exactly you are selling, but I have never wanted to buy something so bad in all of my life. I want to be a part of what you are a part of."

I witnessed firsthand the very thing that Simon Sinek says: *People don't buy what you sell; they buy why you sell it.* The experience was nothing short of magical. When

Chris started on my team, his teammates and I told him that with us, he would *look better, feel better, and make more money!* This was something I had come up with years earlier when asked about my goals for my team. For the next eleven months, Chris never missed his sales target. Chris did indeed look better, feel better, and make a lot more money. Not only that, he accomplished his goal of improving others' perceptions and was promoted to a position in Major Accounts.

Not long after his promotion, I received a letter thanking me for believing in Chris and helping him believe in himself. The letter conveyed genuine gratitude for encouraging him and not giving up. It also stated that Chris had not suffered a single seizure since joining my team. This was something that he never shared with me and really wasn't even sharing now, because the letter wasn't from Chris—it was from his wonderful wife.

His wife took the time to hand-write a note thanking me for leading Chris. She said that everything in their life seemed to be better: Chris's health, their finances, and even their marriage.

After a few more promotions, Chris eventually left the company to pursue his dreams of being an inventor, and was even featured on the television program Shark Tank ™ where he struck a deal with an investor for one of his awesome, life-saving creations. Chris is still a successful business owner today and a very close and valued friend.

Chris's story also illustrates the Secret Formula in action!

Time + Proficiency x Purpose = Game-Changing Results

FIND A WAY TO RALLY!

What happens if you manage a remote team or are over a very large team or organization, spread across cities, states, or even countries? What if you can't "rally?" *Rally* means to gather or assemble, but in this sense, I want you to think of it as a gathering of thoughts, spirit, and purpose. The format you choose is less important if the message behind the purpose is strong enough.

Technology today allows you to communicate in so many ways to different audiences. There are communication and social media applications that are highly efficient, quick, and mobile, and still allow you to express your purpose in a way that is unique and special.

A leader and mutual mentor of mine who works at a very large retail company told me a story about how their COO regularly records video messages of herself and broadcasts them out to the field via an application that is on all their mobile phones. He said that these videos were short, impactful messages of the company's leader expressing gratitude or observations from her travels to the various locations of the company or its vendors. The videos were always shot candidly, by her, wherever she happened to be in the world that day. They were real and honest and not produced or edited by anyone. My friend told me that while he always found the videos good and meaningful, there was one that inspired him and intensified his sense of purpose.

The video came when the company was in the middle of a very large commercial launch of a new product, and while this was great for business, the company found itself understaffed and overcommitted in many areas. While the product launch was a short-term situation, it was a very trying period that had all employees feeling stressed and overwhelmed.

One night in the middle of this launch, at the end of a very long shift, when everyone's stress seemed to be at its peak, a notification rang out from everyone's mobile phones. A new video message had been delivered.

As the weary team members started the message, they noticed something different about their fearless leader. She was a bit more subdued and softer spoken than they had seen, and much to their surprise, she was not wearing any makeup. She had shot the video just a few moments earlier, after an exhausting shift at one of their retail locations.

The COO had spent the shift moving boxes, stocking shelves, and doing any other manual labor that was needed. She had not been there just for the day, but for a week straight. And while she didn't disclose it on the video, the team later learned that she was always the first one there and the last to leave. Now to be fair, the entire staff knew that the company wasn't so short-staffed that the COO *had* to roll up her sleeves to help—in fact, they knew that she *wanted* to roll up her sleeves and help!

Sweaty and makeup-free, against a dimly lit backdrop of a stock room, she explained with a soft tone and big smile how she was very tired and knew that the team was, too. She went on to say that she knew how everyone must be feeling and she didn't want them to think they were in it alone. She said she had worked hard to best prepare the company for a successful rollout but sometimes things happen that you can't plan for. That when things don't go right, flexibility is key, and that sometimes that meant serving in a different capacity than we are used to.

She stated that the company had simply underestimated demand for the new product and the public's willingness to stand in line outside stores for hours, or even overnight, to buy it. As a result, she had failed to align all the resources needed and now, in a tough situation they would need to adapt, be flexible, and overcome, *together*.

She could have shot the video from a hotel room or office, or even been upbeat and told the staff that they needed to be excited as they powered through this difficult time, and so on. Instead, she chose to be vulnerable, authentic, and transparent. She instead chose to show that she was not only human and got tired like anyone else, but that she felt stressed and a bit overwhelmed, too.

She said, "We are in this together and we will get through this together," and she meant it. The team could have blamed her for not adequately planning or for not doing anything else they felt could have been done differently, but they didn't. It was hard to blame her when she had shown them that she was one of them. She had literally put herself in their shoes and dealt with the repercussions of her actions *with* them. She ended the video with a message of optimism, hope, and *togetherness*. She sincerely thanked them, letting them know how much their hard work and dedication meant to her and to the millions of customers they served. This COO, miles away from much of her team, used technology to sincerely rally the team and spread a message of togetherness to the masses.

My friend said that the day prior to that message, he had been in a meeting where it was disclosed that by their calculations, it would take them more than two months to become as operationally sound as they were prior to the product launch, so you can imagine everyone's surprise when they were fully back to normal operations within *two weeks* post-message. This was not an accident or miscalculation based on what they knew before the video. What they didn't count on was what was disclosed to my friend in the weeks following the video.

My friend was told by the teams that the COO had made her purpose crystal clear: to help the team so they could help customers and that they should all do whatever it took to deliver. The team told him that the message was contagious and *inspiring*. The very next day after that message was sent, the teams got to work even earlier, stayed later, and did whatever they could to be as efficient as possible to better serve more customers than in previous days. This single message inspired employees with an overwhelming sense of pride and purpose, coupled with motivation to work hard and implement efficiencies, moved the company to deliver results and recover from a setback weeks, instead of months, ahead of schedule.

NO GIANT IS BUILT ON PURPOSE ALONE. HAVE A PURPOSE AND A PLAN!

Finding and communicating a purpose is vital for building long-term success, but purpose alone will not build giants. You must also develop skills and traits that strengthen whatever business or group of people you serve. You must then become a skill and trait developer yourself, getting your team to invest in themselves and to improve daily. Purpose is critical because it will multiply these efforts, skills, and energy.

Even when you lead with purpose and your people are inspired to achieve greatness, you will still have to design a simple, practical, and repeatable plan around your operations. The best leaders in the world that only have a purpose, rarely achieve the greatness of leaders who have both a purpose *and* a plan. And even if creating a strategy isn't your strong suit, you must at least be able to recognize that one is needed and perhaps hire the types of people to surround you that can put plans in place that support your vision and purpose and that of the organization.

Later, we will cover in detail how to create simple and effective strategies for sustaining the long-term success that directly supports your purpose, but for now, let's look at how you can start identifying and communicating your purpose by discovering how to articulate your beliefs in a leadership philosophy.

APPLICATION FOR LEADING WITH PURPOSE

- Understand and be able to articulate your purpose.
- People will follow you anywhere when they believe how you believe. Surround yourself with others who believe how you believe.
- Recognize that purpose is the force multiplier for everything else, and that with it, you can double or triple efforts and change the game entirely.
- Rally and communicate your purpose to the team in meaningful ways.

GUT CHECK 8: Can you clearly articulate your purpose? Can you help others discover and articulate theirs? Discovering and effectively communicating your purpose will help you align yourself with people who believe how you believe—your people.

△ △ △

GIANT STEP EIGHT: SHARE YOUR LEADERSHIP PHILOSOPHY

Authenticity, expressed openly

"Honesty and transparency make you vulnerable. Be honest and transparent anyway." —Mother Teresa

What if you have a really great vision and purpose but no one hears or remembers it? What are your convictions, your beliefs, the attributes that you strive to achieve? What traits and actions do you expect from your team? Can you, in a few short, impactful statements, state your philosophy on leadership and what it means to you? Can you really *articulate* your purpose? And even if you can, how does your team and your leadership know these things? Think of how much more trust you could build if they did. Think of what a differentiator it could be if you had a single-page document with a message that you could effectively communicate, that would help your team better align around common goals, and that would help prevent conflict and gain you and your team the respect you deserve.

Without transparency, there can be little trust—or even none at all. Without trust, there isn't much of a team. Writing a leadership philosophy will help you authentically and transparently establish and communicate what you stand for and at the same time, be up front about what you expect from others.

The flipside of these expectations is what you *won't* stand for (triggers). Most of us have upset our leader at some point. Do you know how we find out what upsets them? Well, you do said thing and they get upset—the end. But why does it have to be that way? Why can't we as leaders do a better job of informing those around us about what we expect from ourselves and them? We can, and we should.

GUT CHECK 9: If you are reading this and thinking, Oh, my team knows what I expect and what my triggers are, don't believe it—test it! Write down three things you always expect and three things that upset you. Have someone call a member of your team at random and ask them to name these six things, then compare the lists. You may be surprised to hear that your team member couldn't even name most of them, and certainly not all of them. (I won't be.)

If you complete the following short exercises, you will have a document stating your leadership philosophy that is really just a short paragraph on your views and thoughts on leadership, a list of the attributes that you and the team strive for, expectations for both you and them, and triggers or things to avoid. We will cover each of these in detail, but for now, let's focus on the leadership philosophy.

To write a great leadership philosophy, you need to write from your heart and not from your head. You must not overthink this process. In fact, it is critical that you do not put too much thought into it at all, at least at first. The goal is getting your BELIEFS, *feelings, convictions,* and *passions* on paper, so you can refine and clarify them later.

To make it easier, start by answering the following questions. Don't think or hesitate, just answer!

ANSWER THESE QUESTIONS WITH ONLY YOUR GUT RESPONSE:

1. WHY I do what I do is because_____
2. To me, leadership means_____
3. Teamwork and trust are critical because_____
4. As a leader, my words will _____
5. My actions will _____
6. My team and I will focus on _____
7. The goals for my team will be _____
8. As a team, we will_____
9. My team and I will be known for _____
10. I believe in _____

Now, take the time to refine some or all of these finished statements. Make the statements flow from one to the other so they make sense when they are read and presented. Shape them into something that reflects how you look and feel on the inside. In fact, this philosophy you write should be so "you" that if you dropped it in your office and didn't have your name on it, anyone would pick it up and hand it to you, knowing that you wrote it. Then, draft your more final version and continue to refine it.

For reference, I will share my leadership philosophy with you.

MIKEAL R. MORGAN'S LEADERSHIP PHILOSOPHY

"Leadership is my passion, privilege, and life's work. Results oriented but change focused, I will remain focused on changing and improving my own and my team's behaviors, habits, attitudes, and skills to achieve excellence. I will establish and communicate clear goals that stretch us beyond our comfort zones. As a team, we will out-think, out-plan, out-execute and out-everything our competition and our personal best, with integrity. I trust and believe in my team and our ability to change the world. Everything matters, especially the small stuff."

◆ ◆ ◆

Now that you have that down on paper, let's focus on setting the context of the document and the positive attributes, triggers to avoid, expectations, and commitment statement.

Setting the context lets anyone reading it know its intended purpose. Your setting context statement should be found at the top of your leadership philosophy and may sound similar to the following.

SETTING CONTEXT SENTENCE.

The purpose of sharing this document is to give you insight and information on how I think, feel, and act as a leader. It outlines the attributes that my team and I strive to achieve and what we expect from one another, as well as what things to avoid in order to best align our personalities and resources so that we achieve excellence every day. Draft yours now (or just steal mine).

Now, let's tackle the valuable attributes part of the document.

ATTRIBUTES I STRIVE TO ACHIEVE.

Think of "attributes I strive to achieve" as leadership accountability by publicly listing your goals. Here is another way of looking at it: If you had a goal of quitting smoking, think of what happens when you tell everyone at the office about that goal. It makes it very difficult to walk outside without someone asking you if you are going to fail to meet your goal by lighting a cigarette. The same applies when informing the people around you about a diet that you are on. We should publicly announce our goals because it certainly makes it difficult to eat that slice of chocolate cake after announcing the *attributes we are striving to achieve!*

These are the expectations you strive to demonstrate daily. If you were to list the leadership qualities you think are the most valuable and honorable, and that would only be found in a leader whom you would follow anywhere, write them down and ask yourself if you could live up to them. If the answer is *yes*, write them as your valuable attributes. Don't think of a task, but rather the qualities, traits, or features that you aspire to role model. DO NOT PUT SOMETHING THAT DOES NOT DESCRIBE WHAT YOU ARE TRYING TO ACHIEVE. YOUR GOAL IS TO BE AUTHENTIC! WRITE THIS FOR YOU, FIRST!

Here are some positive attributes to get you thinking:

- Integrity
- Faithfulness
- Transparency
- Calmness under pressure
- Compassion
- Passion
- Trustworthiness
- Loyalty
- Responsibility
- Fairness
- Humility
- Self-discipline
- Servitude
- Fearlessness
- Kindness
- Loving attitude
- Reliability
- Approachableness
- _____
- _____
- _____

Once you have selected the attributes that best suit you, come up with a short reason/explanation for why you added it or how you want it to be viewed. I list mine here for reference.

ATTRIBUTES I ASPIRE TO ACHIEVE.

Faith: I am and will always be a believer, first and foremost.

Integrity: I am a principles-based leader and will always say what I mean and mean what I say. Doing things right will never be as important as doing the right thing.

Humility: I am here to humbly out-serve all others I meet.

Work ethic: I do not believe that things just happen, nor do I believe the world owes anyone anything. If we want it, we must go get it.

Professionalism: Everything from punctuality to the shine on my shoes is scrutinized by someone. Each day, I must strive to be my personal best at everything I engage in. In this way, I will differentiate myself from the amateurs. No exceptions. Everything matters.

Passion: I enthusiastically greet each day with a sincere love for what I do, who I am, and my ability to change the world.

Attitude: I am the master of my destiny and will use my positive attitude to overcome even the toughest obstacles. I know that "whether I believe I can or I believe I can't, I'm right."

Accountability: I am responsible and accountable for my actions and words. I do not pass blame. I am accountable for how I make others feel, regardless of intent. I apologize when I am wrong and acknowledge you when you are right.

Servant: I selflessly serve others. I will recognize others for their contributions and achievements by rewarding positive behaviors and results.

Dedication: I will plan my work and work my plan diligently until I succeed. "I will persist until I succeed."

Intelligent utilization of resources: I utilize every support mechanism, system, department, and tool available to deliver the most optimized performance possible.

TRIGGERS TO AVOID.

We discussed earlier the benefits and importance of being transparent with the things that upset or trigger you. Here is where you need to be honest and fair, listing a few of the most important things that should be avoided in order to achieve a great working environment.

Here are some examples of my personal triggers:

- Poor attitude
- Excuses
- Arrogance
- Laziness
- Not controlling the controllable

Record yours now.

TEAM EXPECTATIONS.

Now, decide what expectations from the team are most important to you. The key is to limit this to three to six items. There are a few reasons for this. The first is, if you have too many expectations or if they are too complex, they will simply not be followed. The second reason is more psychological and says to the person reading this completed document that they should expect many things from you as the leader but in return, you only expect a few things from them. This is servant leadership.

For example, I use the Four A's:

- **Attitude**: A great attitude is the starting point for all other greatness.
- **Aptitude**: I encourage everyone to aspire to be the best version of themselves each day. Be true to who you are and play to your strengths. Equally, be self-aware of your opportunities for personal growth and development. Learn, grow, and develop daily.
- **Accountability**: Own your actions and words. Be professional and responsible.
- **Action**: Be dedicated to winning and exceeding expectations with urgency. A bias for action sets the standard against which all others are measured.

Record yours now.

COMMITMENT STATEMENT.

The commitment statement sums up the document and adds a personal element that binds you to it.

Here is what mine looks like:

I will be a dedicated leader, committed to my team, company, and clients. To work hard and intelligently, and enthusiastically lead the team with purpose in executing a well-designed program that clearly outlines our vision, goals, and plan.

Record yours now.

LEADERSHIP STRATEGY.

The final part of this leadership philosophy document is to state your leadership strategy. For the How to Build Giants program, I will outline how the following leadership strategy is effective because I firmly believe that everything you do as a leader could be aligned under one of these three pillars: **People First; Simplify Everything; Inspire Everyone.**

The way these principles align in your organization should change after you have put the How to Build Giants program into place. Whether you are hiring, coaching, reporting—or whatever you do daily as a leader—you do things that ultimately roll up under one of these three pillars. The goal is to better align with this strategy so you can build giants and be the best leader you can be.

THE COMPLETED LEADERSHIP PHILOSOPHY DOCUMENT

Here is an example of my completed, one-page leadership philosophy document. Use your own style and format to present and communicate yours.

Mikeal R. Morgan
Leadership Philosophy

SETTING CONTEXT

The purpose of sharing this document is to give you insight and information on how I think, feel, and act as a leader. It outlines the attributes that my team and I strive to achieve and what we expect from one another, as well as what things to avoid in order to best align our personalities and resources so that we achieve excellence every day.

ATTRIBUTES I ASPIRE TO ROLE MODEL

LEADERSHIP STRATEGY

People First
Simplify Everything
Inspire Everyone

Faith: I am and will always be a believer, first and foremost.

Integrity: I am a principles-based leader and will always say what I mean and mean what I say. Doing things right will never be as important as doing the right thing.

Humility: I am here to humbly out-serve all others I meet.

Work ethic: I do not believe that things just happen, nor do I believe the world owes anyone anything. If we want it, we must go get it.

LEADERSHIP PHILOSOPHY

Leadership is my passion, privilege, and life's work. Results oriented but change focused; I will remain focused on changing and improving mine and my team's behaviors, habits, attitude, and skills to achieve excellence. I will establish and communicate clear goals that stretch us beyond our comfort zones. As a team, we will out-think, out-plan, out-execute and out everything our competition and our personal best, with integrity. I trust and believe in my team and our ability to change the world. Everything matters, especially the small stuff.

Professionalism: Everything from punctuality to the shine on my shoes is scrutinized by someone. Each day, I must strive to be my personal best at everything I engage in. In this way, I will differentiate myself from the amateurs. No exceptions. Everything matters.

Passion: I enthusiastically greet each day with a sincere love for what I do, who I am, and my ability to change the world.

Attitude: I am the master of my destiny and will use my positive attitude to overcome even the toughest obstacles. I know that "whether I believe I can or I believe I can't, I'm right."

Accountability: I am responsible and accountable for my actions and words. I do not pass blame. I am accountable for how I make others feel, regardless of intent. I apologize when I am wrong and acknowledge you when you are right.

Servant: I selflessly serve others. I will recognize others for their contributions and achievements by rewarding positive behaviors and results.

Dedication: I will plan my work and work my plan diligently until I succeed. "I will persist until I succeed."

Intelligent utilization of resources: I utilize every support mechanism, system, department, and tool available to deliver the most optimized performance possible.

TRIGGERS

Poor attitude

Excuses

Arrogance

Laziness

Not controlling the controllable

THE 4 A'S | TEAM EXPECTATIONS

Attitude: A great attitude is the starting point for all other greatness.

Aptitude: I encourage everyone to aspire to be the best version of themselves every day. Be true to who you are and play to your strengths. Equally, be self aware of your opportunities for personal growth and development. In the end, I prefer the errors of enthusiasm to the indifference of wisdom.

Accountability: Own your actions and words. Be professional and responsible.

Action: Dedication to winning and exceeding expectations with urgency. A bias for action and set the standard for all others to be measured against.

MY COMMITMENT

To be a dedicated leader committed to my team, company and clients. To work hard; intelligently and enthusiastically leading the team with a well-designed program that clearly outlines our vision, goals and plan.

"I NEVER LOSE, I EITHER WIN OR I LEARN"
-Nelson Mandela

COMMUNICATING YOUR LEADERSHIP PHILOSOPHY

How you communicate your leadership philosophy is critical. When you email the document, you should make the message simple and state the benefits of having the document in your message. I also print and hang mine in, or around, my office area for a few reasons. For starters, it is what I have told people to expect from me and so when it is visible, it is a nice reminder for me to be the leader I said I would be. Second, my team will reference it for milestones and my ongoing expectations of them. Here is an example of how you could communicate your leadership philosophy in an email:

As a gesture of complete honesty and transparency, I am sending you a copy of my leadership philosophy. In this document, you will find my thoughts and feelings on leadership and how important it is to me. You will also find all the leadership traits that I strive for each day. These are the things for which I openly admit to being responsible and accountable. Along with these expectations of me, you will also find a few expectations I have of all members of the team. The goal of this document is to establish complete clarity of expectations of one another and a deeper level of mutual trust and accountability. The benefits of you having my leadership philosophy are that you will not have to waste time guessing what will make us successful while working together—you will know up front. I would like feedback from you on how you feel about this document and if you feel that anything should be added or removed.

As stated in the email to the team, by effectively communicating your expectations with clarity and transparency, you reduce the time it will take for the team to figure these things out on their own. You are positively contributing to the secret formula and are ultimately able to hold people accountable.

Time + Proficiency x Purpose = Game-Changing Results

By communicating this to the team, you save time every day because your team will not waste time on unimportant things. This gives the team a clear path forward regarding behavior that will contribute to their success. Think of how much time you could have saved in your career if every one of your leaders had provided a document like this to you on day one of working with them.

LIVING YOUR LEADERSHIP PHILOSOPHY.

"Right is right even if no one is doing it and wrong is wrong even if everyone is doing it!" —Saint Augustine

It is one thing to write a leadership philosophy and another thing altogether to live it. Leadership is about doing what is right, not what is easy. Boldly post your leadership philosophy and live up to what you wrote! Wake up each day determined to use it as a guide for your leadership and decisions.

"Nearly all men can stand adversity, but if you want to test a man's character, give him power." —Abraham Lincoln

WILL THEY KNOW YOU BY YOUR SENTENCE?

Peggy Noonan, a *Wall Street Journal* columnist, wrote about the late American politician, ambassador, and wife of the founder of *Time* magazine, Clare Booth Luce, who once told President John Kennedy that, "A great man is one sentence." She went on to say that this means that his leadership can be so well summed up in a single sentence that you don't have to hear his name to know who's being talked about. 'He preserved the union and freed the slaves,' or, 'He lifted us out of a great depression and helped to win a world war.' You didn't have to be told 'Lincoln' or 'FDR.'"

Creating and living your leadership philosophy will help you identify what you stand for and should help you articulate your purpose, but you should be able to condense it so that you can remember it daily. Can you come up with one sentence by which you would like to be remembered? This is similar to writing your own obituary, only shorter and significantly less macabre. You want one sentence that sums you up so that if it were read aloud, your name wouldn't have to be mentioned for people to know who was referenced. This sentence will further help you become accountable and strive for leadership that will literally change people's lives. While mine is a tad vague and isn't as globally impacting as an FDR or Lincoln, I'd like to share it with you anyway:

Boldly leading a life of faith, purpose, and love, so that he leaves a legacy of value.

APPLICATION FOR CREATING A LEADERSHIP PHILOSOPHY

- Identify how you think, feel, and believe about leadership and your team, and record those thoughts.
- Refine those thoughts and put them into a paragraph you could communicate with conviction.
- Identify and record the attributes that you strive to achieve daily, and for which others can hold you accountable.
- Identify and record the triggers or things that should be avoided in order to establish a great working relationship between you and the team.
- Identify and record the most important, few expectations that you have of the team and for which you will hold them accountable.
- Write a commitment statement that binds you to the leadership philosophy that you wrote and the team you serve.
- Communicate the leadership philosophy and use it to better serve and lead the team.
- Live the leadership philosophy and revise it as you grow as a leader.

GUT CHECK 10: I challenge you to stop reading any further until you write your leadership philosophy. Push yourself and do not answer from the head, overthinking each part; rather, answer from the heart and let your true purpose lead you to write what you feel, not what you think! Now, communicate your leadership philosophy so you can be accountable for what others should expect from you. Live this and be the leader you should be, not the one you thought you had to be.

△ △ △

GIANT STEP NINE: LEARN THE STUFF THEY DIDN'T TEACH YOU IN SCHOOL

Sharpening the leadership saw

"Live as if you were to die tomorrow. Learn as if you were to live forever." —*Mahatma Gandhi*

Can leadership be learned, or are great leaders simply born great leaders? Leaders are absolutely made! How well made is entirely up to them. Anyone can be a leader just as anyone can own a pet or be a parent. The thing is, not everyone should own a pet or be a parent, and not everyone should be a leader. Some people may have more capacity to make personal sacrifices, to serve others, and to create other leaders, but even they must still work at it. They study long and hard and are tested often to become great. The question is, what do you study to achieve leadership excellence? What kind of degree should you pursue to ensure you have the right knowledge? What university is the best for leadership development?

What if I told you that they don't have a class for the most important things that leaders need to know? Sure, there are management courses and leadership studies, but I have never seen a listing for a Patience 101 class, or Inspire Others 202, at the local university. In this step of the program, we will explore the most-needed traits, qualities, and skills that all great leaders have, and how you can develop them.

Many of the topics covered in this chapter are, in fact, learned skills. The concern is that if you are not deliberate in your approach to developing both skills and traits, or neglect their development altogether, you will inevitably learn these lessons by the great teachers experience, time, and failure.

Some people become leaders and do a great job of developing others, but end up neglecting their own development. You wouldn't listen to any other professional that stopped learning once they reached a certain point in their career, even if they were really experienced, would you? Would you go to a doctor who has been in practice for thirty years but hadn't studied anything new since med school? Would you hire a CPA who hasn't read tax laws in the last twenty years?

As leaders, we shouldn't work out our leadership muscles simply to keep them from getting weak—we should push ourselves and work the hell out of our leadership muscles to make certain they are strong! We must stretch ourselves and be willing to put the time in to learn, grow, and develop. We can't make excuses. We can't say that because we have the experience we just know something; as leaders, *we can't be concerned with growth—we must be consumed with it!*

"Winners find a way; losers find an excuse." —Gianluigi Buffon

In an impoverished neighborhood in Beaumont, Texas, a young boy who is a bit too concerned with having his shoes stolen off his feet in school to focus much on his studies, grows increasingly frustrated with the school system and life in general. At ten years old, he fails the fourth grade and at thirteen, midway through seventh grade, he drops out of school. There wasn't a lot the boy had learned in school by age thirteen to properly prepare him for the world, and it certainly didn't provide the best foundation for a career in leadership.

He had a had a lot of work to do on core competencies alone, and the fact that he had crippling depression and suicidal thoughts only slowed his efforts. Basic grammar, writing, and mathematics were a struggle and without the structure of school, the struggle lasted for years.

Making his situation more complex, he also became a father at seventeen, further limiting his time to pursue formal education or to even study in the conventional sense. In response, he became unconventional and determined. With a child on the way, he found purpose. Each night, while his friends partied, he too stayed up late, but instead of partying, he read. In the early morning, while everyone else slept, he read.

He stayed the course and all the way through his twenties, while growing his family and his career, his appetite for growth and development strengthened to the point that he was reading at least a book a week. He understood that true development meant reading more than a book a week, though. He paid attention and worked at as many places as he could, strengthening his knowledge through the diversity of experience and development. While working at restaurants, he learned to speak Spanish from Spanish-speaking employees in exchange for teaching them English. He learned to build websites by networking with web developers, watching videos, and practicing and failing a lot. He attended seminars and joined local groups to improve his ability to communicate and speak publicly.

He could have made excuses and said that having two or three jobs and supporting his young family left him no time to develop at this pace, but he was driven by something bigger than himself. He made the time and found his purpose and gained the proficiency that would eventually change the game.

Time + Proficiency x Purpose = Game-Changing Results

The man in this example happens to be me. The first high school I ever stepped foot inside was the one where I registered my son as a student. The only time I have been on a university campus were the times I was a keynote speaker. While I am not proud that I gave up on school, I am proud that I never gave up on education. And while I have not ruled out pursuing a formal education, I also no longer harbor feelings of guilt for not having a degree.

"I have never let my schooling interfere with my education."

—Mark Twain

Formal or informal, leaders must be learners and should *make time* to develop themselves and others. This is something you must plan and even budget for. It should also be formally scheduled, in order to make the time available. As leaders, we should have the mindset to make the investment in development now, so that we secure victory in the future. Leaders focus on winning the entire war, not just today's battle.

"If your plan is for one year, plant rice. If your plan is for ten years, plant trees. If your plan is for one hundred years, educate children."
—Confucius

MY STUDY OF WHAT LEADERS NEED MOST TO BE SUCCESSFUL.

Over the course of ten years, I asked more than a thousand people the same question: *What things make the greatest leaders, great?* And for ten years, I have captured the same results over and over again with very little variance, regardless of the respondent's cultural background, country of origin, gender, age, or race. Here are my top five findings, in priority order:

1. Integrity (T)
2. Ability to inspire (T)
3. Puts people first (T)
4. Emotionally intelligent (T/S)
5. Great communicator (S)

After gathering this information, I then asked each respondent to mark each of their responses with a (T) for trait, if this was not a learned skill (something you couldn't take a class for), and to mark it with an (S) for skill, if it was a characteristic that could be learned. One fact holds true: eighty percent or more were not categorized as learned skills, but as a trait, quality, or behavior. Some might qualify as both. For instance, there are many things that you can learn that can help you develop emotional intelligence , but at its core, it still ends up being more of a quality that one chooses or has the ability to demonstrate consistently.

My decade-long study further supported my belief that the most important things needed in order to be an effective leader are not taught in school, but through life's hard lessons.

The work that is required to be the best can seem overwhelming, so don't bite off more than you can chew; instead, work on one thing a time until you have hit significant achievement milestones. Keep in mind that some of the development you will need to take on must be accomplished through practice or even through trial and error. Some traits may take years to develop and require continuous attention, and all of them will require a conscious effort. (Side note: I did find it interesting that intelligence ranked sixth, behind these other things, including being a great communicator.)

YOU ARE ALL THAT YOU CONSUME.

You have probably heard the saying, "You are what you eat." But what about what you hear and see? How about your environment? You are, in fact, everything that you consume on a broad scale.

Everything around you, from what kind of music you listen to, to which people you listen to, shapes you. You are a product of all that you consume. Be very selective with all things that you consume and ensure that you consume only those things that bring you peace, education, joy, inspiration, health, and balance. Even one toxic friend or one negative influence could be enough to put you at an imbalance. You owe it to yourself and are obligated to your team to safeguard your consumption and to ensure that it is wholesome.

Take stock in what you do daily and figure out if it is good, bad, or "just there."

Pass the people and things in your life through the following filters:

o	Adds value to me	o	Challenges me to be better
o	Makes me happy	o	Cheers me up
o	Makes me better	o	Is healthy
o	Relaxes me	o	Is useful
o	Helps me think	o	Is legal

Everything you consume should fulfill at least three things on this list. If you are having a hard time justifying something, you should probably limit its consumption. Chocolate cake or alcohol might cheer you up, but if you have to stretch too far or have a hard time choosing a third filter, you should probably not stretch it to the point of saying that it "helps you think" and simply limit how much you consume. Cake isn't a bad thing, but too much cake is. Balance is key. Don't consume what you don't want to become.

BE CURIOUS, PART ONE: CURIOSITY KILLED THE CAT BUT FAVORED THE LEADER.

Being *naturally* curious as a leader allows you to learn an incredible amount about your people, business, and clients, all in an innocent manner. Being naturally curious allows you to be put in scenarios of trust and confidence that being a leader alone might prevent you from accessing. Being naturally curious allows you to discover the root causes of issues and problems that hinder success.

You must be willing to allow yourself to be put into these situations, though, because being nosy or approaching situations with the wrong intentions is very different from simply being curious. Constantly checking up on and micro-managing people erodes trust and makes people not like you.

Many leaders start this journey of natural curiosity but quickly become like an overzealous child who asks a question and then proceeds to answer to impress others with what they know or think they know. The almost instant agreement this will elicit from your people will come from a place of position and not truth, and while it might boost your enormous ego, it does nothing to bolster your knowledge of anything or show the team that you care or want their knowledge or expertise. In fact, this behavior can quickly damage your personal brand.

I witnessed a man in a director-level position at a very large organization approach a data entry supervisor, more than four levels below him on the organizational chart, with hopes of identifying why there was such a large backlog of unprocessed work orders. The interaction started off fine as they exchanged general pleasantries. The director was naturally curious and while he was sincere, he was very specific about his displeasure with the delays, and the interaction very quickly transitioned an interrogation. The supervisor, visibly embarrassed, said that they had simply fallen behind and were working as quickly as they could, and that they expected to be caught up any day now. The director, seemingly satisfied, later reported to his staff that he had personally addressed the backlog issue and that it would be resolved within a day or so. What the director got was the answer he wanted, but not the one he needed.

The following day, I approached the same supervisor and explained that I had witnessed the interaction and that I was curious if my team could be of any assistance to her and her team. She explained that the system has suffered a server failure and that all the work orders had to be processed manually. She said that she was too overwhelmed by the director's approach and demeanor to explain that to him. She said that she felt it was better to just "fall on the sword" and take personal responsibility for the backlog. Her greater concern was that the server issues would continue and she would have to push her team even harder to compensate.

BE CURIOUS, PART TWO: ENCOURAGE CANDOR.

Sure, there is an opportunity here to coach the supervisor about her ability to communicate the root cause, but I go back to the fact that maybe it's an "us problem."

It could be that no one informed the director that there were server issues, for example. Most companies, especially large ones, have lost the ability to have true candor and instead yield to the "yes-man mentality." It's true that accountability is a great leadership tool, but if you aren't identifying—let alone addressing—the root cause, you more than likely aren't holding the right things or people accountable. Be naturally curious and stop looking for *who* and start looking for *why*. After all, do you want to be great or do you want to be right?

ASKING GREAT QUESTIONS, PART ONE: WE ARE JUDGED MORE ON THE QUALITY OF THE QUESTIONS WE ASK THAN THE ANSWERS WE GIVE.

People are naturally drawn to a leader who stimulates them intellectually and makes them feel valued. People want a leader who makes them think, wonder, dream, and believe. People also want to be listened to and really heard.

Great leaders use great questions to accomplish this. If you have done a great job of hiring, (a skill we talk about later in this program) and you have hired a quality person, you need to challenge that person to think and dream, not once, but as often as possible. You must get great at asking great questions.

Great leaders who have mastered this have a few things going for them. First, they have a bank of questions that fit the various situations they face regularly. These questions are very well thought out, unique, and invoke deep thought and can be adapted to fit a wide range of situations.

These questions are open ended and not true or false, test-type questions and thus do not put the respondent on the spot. Putting people on the spot will cause uncomfortable situations and lead people to avoid you at all costs. Again, the goal of the questions is to make people think and to feel valued, not to make them uncomfortable. The information they provide in their answers is a bonus.

Second, great leaders understand when to ask great questions and are not afraid to get truthful answers. They listen carefully, withholding judgment, emotion, or even facial expressions that would reveal their thoughts or opinions on where the questions take the conversation.

Finally, great leaders understand that while they may not agree with an answer, or even understand why they get the answers they do, the information they get holds some value, if not immediately, perhaps in the future or when combined with additional details. As leaders, we must understand that people's perception is truly their reality, whether we like it or not.

THE ELEVATOR RIDE: ASKING GREAT QUESTIONS, PART TWO.

The CEO of a large call center found herself in an elevator with a frontline employee in an encounter that would reshape the way the company did business. The CEO frequently rode the elevator when she knew frontline employees would be there and used the time to get what she called "real talk."

One day, she found herself with a quiet, petite young lady who stood in the back of the elevator, avoiding eye contact with the CEO at all costs. The CEO smiled and said, "What is the very best part of your job?" The employee slowly looked up and with a huge smile, answered, "When I take a call from an upset caller and turn them around, making them happy. I feel a sense of accomplishment." The employee went on to say, "I know I am doing a good job when that happens."

The CEO smiled and thanked her, then asked, "What is the dumbest thing we do here at this company?" She followed up with, "Is there something we can do to make it less dumb?"

When I interviewed this CEO as part of my research for this program, she told me that this elevator ride reshaped the way the company measured the success of their frontline employees. The young lady on the elevator that day told her about how the success metrics were outdated and actually conflicted with the company's vision of putting clients first.

In that short ride, the CEO learned something that a dozen focus groups, weekly staff meetings, and four employee surveys couldn't or wouldn't reveal. After being bold enough to make the suggested changes, the company realized a twenty-two percent increase in employee retention and drove center productivity up over thirty-three percent the following year. This clearly shows how your ability to ask a great question at the right time and in the right situation can help you be a better leader—that is, if you truly listen and are willing to act on what you learn.

ALWAYS RESPOND, NEVER REACT.

"Give me six hours to chop down a tree and I'll spend the first four sharpening the axe."—Abraham Lincoln

From a communication perspective, is one better than another? By definition, both *respond* and *react* mean to "reply to something in a particular way." While similar, the difference is in the "a particular way" part! Responding, more deeply defined, is about taking in and digesting information before intelligently providing a response. The reply is well thought out and planned. Reacting, more deeply defined, typically happens faster, is less thought out and is more based on emotion or initial perception rather than fact or circumstance.

At a seminar in the late '90s, I watched the late, great Zig Ziglar explain the difference between responding and reacting. Zig was a world-renowned motivational speaker and trainer who spoke on topics including sales, faith, marriage, and leadership, to name a few.

At this seminar, he spoke on leadership and explained how reacting and responding are not only different, but that reacting in most situations is a bad thing and not limited to communication. Zig explained that if someone who was ill took medication and subsequently broke out into hives, the doctor would treat them for an allergic *reaction*—a bad thing. Conversely, if someone took medication for an illness and their condition improved, the doctor might remark that the patient *responded* to the treatment—a good thing. As leaders, reacting is seldom, if ever, appropriate.

In situations where most people have the natural impulse to react, strong leaders will resist this urge and instead *respond*, with urgency, if warranted.

This is especially true where physical danger is present. When a building is on fire and people must be evacuated safely, reactions could result in injuries or worse. You will often hear in emergency preparedness meetings that the very first thing that must be accomplished in any emergency is for everyone to remain calm. After all, during an emergency, who would follow a leader who is freaking out and screaming for everyone to run for their lives?

Instead, a leader responding with urgency will, if possible, calmly rely on prior planning that outlines where and how people should safely evacuate. If there was no prior planning, a leader who responds would find an evacuation map that shows the route to move people calmly to safety.

Reacting sometimes causes panic, and panic sometimes leads us to react. Either way, panic causes irrational thoughts that cause irrational behaviors, and that is just bad.

Think through all situations and always consider the long-term implications. Reacting is typically very, very short term, while responding means thinking through the here and now and considering what will happen after the next three steps are taken. As a leader, when you are put in situations where you can respond or react, ask yourself what will happen after the next three things I am planning on doing here? This typically gets you thinking and responding versus emotionally reacting to the situation.

After all, when it comes to real life-or-death scenarios, law enforcement, firefighters, and emergency medical services are called first "responders" and not first "reactors" for a reason.

ACTIVELY LISTEN.

"A leader who can speak ten languages isn't nearly as impactful as a leader who can listen in one." —Anonymous

One of the biggest opportunities leaders have is in listening. Listening is such an important skill that you should strive to show continuous, daily improvement in your ability to effectively listen.

While there are classes and books on listening, I listed it here because it is a skill that is simple to grasp but difficult to apply. Here are a few things that I have studied for several years that help me be a better listener and that I still practice every day:

"It's not what you communicate; it's what gets communicated." —Anonymous

- Give the speaker your full and uninterrupted attention. Have no electronics beeping and buzzing to take your attention away from their message.
- Remain genuinely curious about what the other person is talking about.
- Do not have a bias. Leave opinions and judgment out, at least until you have listened to all of what someone is saying and how they are saying it.
- Listen to more than just the words. The ability to effectively read body language is critical. People will make certain movements, use their hands or arms in certain ways, make faces and use many nonverbal cues that add to what they are trying to communicate. We must pay attention to the words that others say and how they choose to say them if we want complete communication.
- Don't simply wait for your turn to talk. I have rarely had conversations end so abruptly that I don't have a chance to respond. It is important to listen intently until it is your chance and the time is right. We must learn to be patient enough to wait until the speaker pauses and looks for a response.
- Don't assume you know the answer or could fully complete their sentence, with their same perspective. Even if you know what the other person is going to say, you need to listen for their unique perspective, which could shed new light on the situation.
- Perspective in verbal communication is as important as punctuation and spelling is in written communication. It's the difference in knowing you're shit and knowing your shit. It's how the comma can make the difference between life and death: Let's eat grandma, or let's eat, grandma! When you listen and really understand the other person's perspective, you will have a more complete understanding of what the other person says.

"Leaders that who don't listen will eventually find themselves surrounded by people with nothing to say." —Andy Stanley

STOP MULTI-TASKING! LEADERS GIVE UNDIVIDED ATTENTION.

Most people who are self-professed multi-taskers will tell you that they are effective and can handle juggling multiple things at once. In addition, multi-tasking has become very appealing, primarily because of today's numerous digital distractions. There have been many studies on the subject of multi-tasking, and most show one thing to be true: when a person does more than one thing at a time, they do all of those things with less quality and precision.

In his book *Emotional Intelligence 2.0*, Travis Bradberry shares his thoughts and extensive research on how multi-tasking can kill productivity and even harm your brain.

Even if you don't think the research on the topic is sound, multi-tasking around your team or clients is simply rude. If you are meant to give attention to someone else and you glance down at your phone or computer screen, you are doing both you and the team member a disservice. Pay attention to your people and give them the respect they deserve. The return on the investment of uninterrupted time is almost certain to pay huge dividends in productivity and respect.

There is no magic bullet other than to just stop trying to do more than one thing at a time. Give people your full attention when speaking to them. To avoid feeling the need to multi-task, set the right expectations up front. If you have to leave or are otherwise occupied, let that person know that to be fair to you both and to give that person your complete attention, you will set aside time when both of you are available.

CHALLENGE THE STATUS QUO.

Every time I think about the status quo, I am reminded of the old story about five monkeys. The story goes like this:

A scientist put five monkeys in a cage, strung a bunch of ripe bananas from the top of the cage and positioned a ladder directly underneath the bananas. Before long, one of the monkeys climbed the ladder. As soon as the monkey neared the top of the ladder, the scientist rushed in and sprayed all the monkeys with cold water.

Time after time, the monkeys were sprayed with cold water. Eventually, when another monkey attempted to climb the ladder, the other monkeys tried to prevent it.

The scientist then removed one monkey and replaced it with a new one. The new monkey saw the bananas and began climbing the ladder. Much to the new monkey's dismay, all the other monkeys attacked him. The more the new monkey attempted, the more the other monkeys fought back.

Next, the scientist removed another of the original five monkeys and replaced it with a new one. The newest monkey attempted to retrieve the bananas and like the other new monkey, he, too, was attacked. The previous newcomer even took part in the attack, as well. The same behavior was exhibited as the third, fourth, and fifth original monkeys were replaced with new ones.

Most of the monkeys attacking the newest member had no clue why they were not allowed to climb the ladder and eat the bananas, or why they participated in the attack on the newest monkey.

None of the five new monkeys had ever been sprayed with cold water. Still, none of them attempted to climb the ladder to retrieve the bananas, and they didn't even know why. They didn't attempt it because it's always been that way!

While that story has been told for years, it's not likely that the experiment ever actually happened. But the "herd mentality" it illustrates is real. The idea of a group mind (or herd mentality or mob behavior) was first published by French social psychologists Gabriel Tarde and Gustave Le Bon in the early 1900s. Other studies in human and animal behavior show how we, like other animals, behave similarly, doing or not doing the same things for years and years with little explanation, understanding, or questioning of the status quo, just because others do it or because that is the way it's always been.

Do not get caught in the herd mentality. Instead, ask *why not* to push the boundaries of what is possible and stop thinking about what isn't possible. Review rules, policies, and procedures that may be very outdated or no longer serve a real purpose. Adopt technology and look to improve the time your team spends on tasks. **I will reiterate a point I made earlier:**

The seven most expensive words in business: "We have always done it that way."

THE LEADERSHIP PIT STOP.

As a leader, you move at a fast pace; you have high stress and make tough decisions. You have people depending on you to know a lot, do a lot, and be everywhere at all times. How do you manage to burn brightly without burning out? I have stated several times in this book that leaders should get up earlier or stay up later if need be to completely serve others, and that leaders are not lazy and should not hit the snooze button, and so on.

That said, even very strong people are not always able to move as fast as most leaders are required to move, and work the hours that leaders are expected to work, while carrying the weight of the world on their shoulders and while also staying happy and healthy for any long period of time. As you do in so many leadership decisions, you must decide if you are going to risk your long-term results on short-term gains.

I call this "Pit Stop Syndrome." Leaders, like race car drivers, must decide when the optimal time is to take a break, refuel, and prepare to finish the race. And like some leaders, some race car drivers too intent on pushing the limits put their car, their health, and the race at risk for the sake of time or stubbornness.

Pit stops, while causing you to lose time at that moment, better prepare you to carry on further, better, and safer. For the race car driver, this means simple things like hydration, fuel, tires, and other small directions and correction. For a leader, the things needed are more or less definitive and are determined by each leader in his or her own unique situation. Needs can vary greatly depending on the industry you are in and how long it has been since your last pit stop.

Sure, sometimes risks pay off and not making a pit stop pays off, but at what cost? For race car drivers, it is usually the cost of replacing an engine that is no longer safe or is ruined from overuse. But for a leader, what are the costs? Are they as definitive?

Did pushing the limits and not taking a pit stop cause the trust to erode between you and a team member? Did you damage your brand for the sake of a deadline or small achievement?

Most people think of leading as giving direction, but leadership is as much about taking direction as it is about giving it. As leaders, we must learn to stop, *be still* and listen, and take direction. Taking direction doesn't just mean listening to other individuals, but taking stock in the environment, current or changing circumstances, the talent of the team, timelines, goals, and any gaps anticipated in the plan. You must also pay close attention to the signs (like pain) your body sends you.

Taking time to look at a map doesn't mean you are lost; sometimes it's important to stop and look at the map to ensure you are still on the right track.

By being strategic and resting, you gain a perspective that cannot be gained while running at full speed. Take the time to make leadership pit stops. Your body, your team, and your goals will thank you. And if you don't think that you have time to take a break for wellness, just wait until your body fails and you are forced to take a break for illness. Forced breaks never come at the right time, typically keep you away from the action longer, and are usually much costlier.

CAN YOU ASK YOURSELF THE BALANCE QUESTION?

"Balance is not something you find, it's something you create."

—Jana Kingsford

Maintaining balance as a human, let alone a leader, may be one of the hardest things to do on the planet. Being still long enough to rest and evaluate things is a big step toward maintaining balance as a leader, but you will still need to learn to ask the balance question.

As a leader, ask yourself if there is a balance in how hard you push people and how hard you allow them to push themselves. Ask yourself if there is a balance in how often you make decisions and how often you give others autonomy to make them. Do you have balance in terms of how much time you spend with family and how much time you spend at work? Is there balance in spending time developing yourself versus developing others?

The list goes on forever in terms of balance in leadership, parenting, working, playing, and so on. The first step you must take in order to achieve balance is to simply ask yourself if there is balance. To look at whatever you are doing and ask yourself if the scales are balanced. If they are not, you must take the most critical step in creating balance: having the fortitude to stop making excuses and to do your very best to balance the proverbial scales. Without this ability to stop and ask yourself the balance question, you run the risk of your entire life becoming—and staying—out of balance.

BE DECISIVE.

"Some people are very decisive when it comes to not making decisions." —Brendan Francis

As a leader, you have people and results depending on you and your ability to make decisions. Leaders who are willing to be bold and make mistakes are more decisive and typically more successful that those who hesitate or procrastinate.

Decision-making can be difficult depending on the nature of the decisions. For instance, larger-scale decisions, such as deciding to terminate employees or changing your business model, require more thought, process, collaboration, and time. No one is expecting snap decisions on these types of issues. The daily decisions on small things are what usually hold up many businesses and frustrate teams.

Determine if your decision-making process could improve and be faster. And just because no one has told you that you suck at making good decisions quickly, doesn't mean that you don't have an issue. While most people who are honest with themselves could tell you if they have a problem in this area, some do not, so invest the time to find out the extent of any concern with you or in your organization.

Next, if the decisions are definitive things that can be measured, develop a simple, effective process that will help you decide faster. Use scales, certain data factors, or other analytics that use an "if this, then this" logic.

THE BROKEN RULER.

When decisions can't be made swiftly, business stalls, and that is dangerous for many reasons. If you have definitive things that can determine an outcome but you or other leaders hesitate to call the shots, then I suggest using a ruler, even if that ruler is broken.

For years as a leader in an outside sales organization, I watched salespeople and leaders argue over specific account ownership. There was constant quarreling over where the account made its decisions, where it primarily operated from, or what industry the account was most a part of. One website claimed one thing or at other times wouldn't provide clarity at all. Other times, one rep would have an email directly from the client stating one thing or another as proof of ownership. Truths and lies were traded and the real facts of the account ownership lay somewhere in between.

Frustration ran high and the culture deteriorated. It wasn't until a new director, Seth Hachmeister took over the sales department that this all changed. Seth was a dedicated leader that worked hard and cared about people, culture and productivity. Seth listened and paid attention as the arguments over account ownership escalated daily. Sales managers lined up in his office, with file folders, printed emails, and website descriptions to plead their cases. Seth knew that this petty arguing was hurting productivity and morale and was killing business.

Instead of making a thousand individual decisions, he made one broad decision: all account ownership would be determined by the company's client-relationship management system, since this was what leadership initially used to determine quotas, team headcount, total available opportunities, and other decisions to begin with.

Almost instantly, the sales managers argued about the system's inaccuracies and unreliable information. Seth stood firm, claiming that even if the information was bad, is was consistently bad. He went on to say that he realized the ruler was broken but that every team would use the same *broken ruler*.

As absurd as that sounded at the moment, I understood that he accomplished a few things here. One, a strategic decision was made. His large-scale, overarching decision helped him avoid having to personally make thousands of small decisions, saving hours each day. Two, he put a system in charge so that you couldn't be mad at another sales manager if a decision didn't go your way. You could only be mad at a system, and therefore the personal attacks stopped.

Was this a perfect decision? I am not sure any decisions are, but this one at least resolved the internal fighting. Over the next several months, the fighting stopped and morale improved dramatically. Our internal turnover of salespeople was reduced by over fifteen percent. Sales skyrocketed, realizing gross gains of nearly thirty percent in only six short months.

People became less concerned with fighting and more concerned with selling. He eliminated the confusion and gave people clear and direct instruction on what they should and shouldn't focus on. This gave us all the ability to hold everyone accountable.

THE GREY AREA.

If decisions are based on less-conclusive facts, or in the "grey area," some organizations use deadlines to tighten the process or even form a committee to render a decision by the end of their meeting, or something similar.

Emotion and "gut feelings" will come into play as well when making decisions. This isn't always a bad thing, as some decisions should evoke emotion and that emotion should be used in the process. Other times, it should be avoided altogether. There is a quote that explains how to use a catalyst to discover your "gut feeling" when making decisions:

"When you have to make a hard decision, flip a coin. Because when that coin is in the air you suddenly know what you're hoping for."
—Anonymous

To me, this quote just means that right or wrong, a lot of times we know what we really want and just need a catalyst to help us realize it. Some additional logic to keep in mind when emotion enters the decision-making process is: "Never make decisions when you are sad or angry, and never make promises when you are happy." Using this logic will help prevent you from making decisions entirely off emotion.

Decision-making can be lonely and difficult (leadership often is), but the bottom line is to choose a method and be decisive.

"Be decisive. Right or wrong, make a decision. The road of life is paved with flat squirrels who couldn't make a decision"
—Anonymous

KNOW WHEN TO HAVE PATIENCE.

When I bought my first home, I was determined to make it the best-looking house on the block. I carefully landscaped the front yard, adding a stone-lined garden directly in the front for all to see. I covered every square inch of the garden with colorful plants. At the same time, my next-door neighbor was determined that he would take the honor of best-looking lawn on the block. He built a slightly larger garden, edged the grass perfectly, and planted even more colorful flowers than I did.

Both of our gardens looked amazing. That is, as long as you stood on the sidewalk directly in front of them. You see, all the plants my neighbor and I planted were young and not quite tall enough to peak over the stone border, so they were impossible to see from the roadway. At the end of the day when we both did all of our planting, I noticed my neighbor hop in his car. When he returned, he carried into the house a giant bottle of fertilizer. I thought to myself, *no way he is going to get his garden bigger, faster than I can.*

The next day I was at the store buying fertilizer, determined to rush this whole plant-growing process. I looked on the back of the bottle and the directions that clearly said to use one tablespoon of fertilizer per gallon of water, and to mix this thoroughly and spread evenly on top of the plants. One gallon covered a ten-foot-square area. I thought to myself, *if one tablespoon is good, I'll bet a couple of cups of this magic juice mixed in a gallon of water will have these plants over the top of those stones in no time!* Even if you aren't a gardener, you can probably guess what happened.

My garden burned up within about two days, causing me to have to rip out all the dead vegetation and start over. I even had the added cost of buying more dirt to mix with the existing dirt so I wouldn't repeat my hurried disaster of over-fertilization.

While fertilizer can help a plant grow faster (if used in moderation), the process, like the growth process of humans, takes time and good conditions to grow properly and safety. We must learn and practice patience in instances where time is required for proper results.

At other times, those who wait get left behind. I encourage all leaders to have enough patience when spending time up front that will benefit the end-result, such as evaluating situations that could be dangerous. You should exercise patience when evaluating plans that you have developed. If you are executing well and circumstances haven't drastically changed, have patience and give your plans a chance to work. I have seen many leaders change direction or the entire company's direction before their plans ever had a chance to work.

Exercise patience when developing people, allowing for mistakes without growing angry. Remember, time and experience are great teachers.

On the flip side, I also encourage you not to exercise patience in cases when not acting with urgency could cost you in the future. Never wait just to wait; instead, have a bias toward action.

INTELLIGENT UTILIZATION OF RESOURCES.

"Make sure that you always have the right tools for the job.
It's no use trying to eat a steak with a teaspoon, and a straw."
—Anthony T. Hincks

In the introduction I used the example of Roger Banister and how he is credited with being the first person ever recorded to have run a mile in under four minutes, and how since his triumph, this feat is regularly accomplished, even by kids in high school. The primary reason for the accomplishment in 1954 was the belief that it was possible. The secondary reasons I believe were training, conditioning, and the intelligent utilization of resources. The reason high school athletes are accomplishing this speed today has to do with what they are being taught from years of experience, the technology used to track, monitor, and enhance training, as well as advancements in areas like nutrition. People who intelligently use these resources to prepare mentally, physically, and nutritionally are better prepared to run and to win. Like running, business and life can be made better by intelligently using your available resources.

How are you evaluating all the resources available to you and your team? Are you consistently seeking new and better resources? Is your team *properly* using the resources they have at their disposal? Are they using the allocated resources at all?

There is a photo that floats around the internet that perfectly illustrates the point of underused and misused resources. It shows a man at a baseball game. He is facing the sun and has his hand placed in sort of a saluting position to shield his eyes. Not weird, except for the fact that he is wearing a baseball cap (backwards) and has sunglasses perched on top of the hat. This man is using his hand when he literally has two different tools designed for the specific purpose of shielding him from the sun, with better results.

Underutilization of resources often happens when technology is introduced to assist with process improvement and automation. Some technology is too complex for the user to benefit from or the user isn't properly trained to effectively use the resource. In either cases, the resource, while introduced with good intentions, will go unused. In other cases, when a new technology resource is deployed, people's natural reluctance to change interferes with its utilization. As leaders, we must be able to identify and address these realities so that the team has everything it needs to be successful.

While we have only described resources as tools that people should know about, understand, and have access to, resources are not limited to these things. Resources can also be people, as well as knowledge and other intangibles.

To determine what resources are needed and preferred, I ask my team the magic wand question to determine how close I can get to what they need with available resources. The question is this: "Understanding that the goal of the task at hand is X, if you had a magic wand, what resources would you create to help you achieve the goal?" I am careful to ask questions about how, when, and why the resources are needed if I don't fully understand. In some cases, the team identifies a resource that I have readily available and in other cases I am forced to create, find, or procure it. If a required resource is already available, ensure that the team is properly trained and fully understands it before checking it off your to-do list.

To ensure your team has the available resources needed to be successful, follow these recommendations:

1. Frequently solicit feedback from your team about what resources are needed, as tasks, people, and goals shift over time.
2. Ensure that the resources are simple and understood. Some resources, especially technology, will require training and reinforcement to be effective.

3. Ensure that the resources are used and used correctly.

4. Think creatively about what resources you could provide the team that they may not know to ask for. Remember that resources can be people or intangible things such as information.

5. Be careful not to introduce too many resources at one time. Instead, focus on getting people properly trained on a resource, if required.

6. Know when a resource should be rolled and when it should be sold. Some leaders spend precious capital on resources that are never used because the team never understands the benefit of having them. These are the resources that must be sold to the team. Put together a quick video, training, or promo announcement that makes clear how the new resource will help the team. Most resources will help the team do something bigger, better, faster, or smarter; the key is getting the team to understand.

EMOTIONAL INTELLIGENCE: EQ

"Emotional intelligence is the ability to sense, understand, and effectively apply the power and acumen of emotions as a source of human energy, information, connection, and influence." —Robert K. Cooper, Ph.D.

A manager held a meeting to discuss his team's underwhelming performance. He was visibly upset, even angry. He pounded his fists on the boardroom table in frustration, certain that the poor performance was due to his team's poor adoption of the company's new computer systems.

"Why is it that you people can't get the hang of the new computer program?" he yelled. It was so simple . . . for him.

One of the women in the group explained how the computer program worked fine but that the computers themselves lagged and had poor connectivity, causing delays that hampered productivity. The manager, now enraged, said that was just an excuse and that they weren't buying new computers.

After the meeting, people filed out one by one with their heads hung low, only to return to their desks to discover that the manager had already fired off a scathing email threatening disciplinary action if the team didn't stop making excuses and improve immediately.

Maybe this manager did have a people problem, but even if he did, it is unlikely that the problem involved every member of his team. This manager's reactionary and accusatory behavior underscored his lack of emotional intelligence.

And maybe you read that and thought, *Man, that guy sounds like an asshole. I'd never do that to my people!* And maybe you haven't gone as far as calling people out and pounding your fists, but when things aren't going your way, if you aren't looking first at your own actions, resources, or lack thereof, or even the quality of resources offered, as well as other factors that could be to more to blame than your people, you may want to sharpen your EQ skillset.

This is just one example of a lack of EQ. There are many ways that a lack of EQ manifests, including:

- Never accepting the blame or considering that it may be a *"you"* problem.
- Becoming easily stressed and staying that way for long periods of time.
- Having difficulty "reading the room" or an individual's body language.
- Not being able to communicate or express many emotions other than frustration or anger.
- Having difficulty telling people you are proud of them.
- Not getting a lot of jokes or not finding many things amusing.
- Displaying expectant or ungrateful behaviors.
- Not being curious.
- Thinking you know everything, and that others have very little to add in terms of benefits.
- Being quick to criticize others.
- Being scared to try new things or being extremely fearful of change.
- Not being able to see bigger-picture issues or lacking vision.

EQ typically increases with age and experience for most people. But young or old, you can improve if you are first honest enough with yourself and do some serious introspection. To make corrections, work on it consistently by involving other leaders who are willing to provide coaching to address the symptoms listed above.

There are thousands of books written about EQ that break down the *what* and *how* of emotional intelligence, but like so many topics, just because it is simple, doesn't mean it's easy.

"When dealing with people, remember you are not dealing with creatures of logic, but with creatures of emotion."
—Dale Carnegie

WHAT SIZE SHOE DO YOU WEAR? EMPATHY.

"When you show deep empathy toward others, their defensive energy goes down, and positive energy replaces it. That's when you can get more creative in solving problems."—Stephen Covey

Mastering empathy will multiply a leader's effectiveness exponentially. As leaders, we must be able to put ourselves in the shoes of others and do our best to understand things from their perspective. It is through empathy that respect, dedication, and admiration build, and people become connected to a leader at a deeper level. When your team understands that you deeply care about them, and that you have their best interests at heart, they will be motivated to do more for you and the business.

Here is an example of how a situation could be handled by two different leaders, one who shows empathy and one who doesn't.

Scenario:

A team member is thirty minutes late for work. This individual is a good member of the team—not the most productive and not the least. They have been late once or twice in the last twelve months. When the leader looks at the clock and notices that the team member isn't there, they call the team member's mobile phone. The team member answers and is noticeably upset, breathing hard and explaining in a loud voice that they know they are late. Their car broke down in the middle of the freeway.

Leader 1: "First of all, don't raise your voice at me, I'm not the one late for work— you are. Second, ensuring that your car is in good working condition is your responsibility. I need you here at the office as soon as possible." Hangs up.

Leader 2: "Oh my—that's awful! First of all, are you okay?"

Team member: "Yes, and I'm sorry I am yelling. This is just the worst day ever."

Leader 2: "Are you in a safe place off of the roadway and have you called a tow truck?"

Team member: "Yes, thank you. I am off to the side of the road and yes, I called for a tow truck."

Leader 2: "Can I come get you and take you somewhere?"

Team member: "Wow, that is kind of you, but no. I will call for a ride but I am not sure what to do with my car and so I don't know what time I can make it in to the office."

Leader 2: "Don't worry about that; for now, take care of yourself, and your car and call me later. If you need anything in the meantime, call and I will do whatever I can to help."

I don't think it took you too long to figure out which of these leaders showed empathy and as a result will be more effective. Leader 1 may have gotten the team member to come to work that day, but at what cost? How productive will that person be that day? How will they feel about the leader going forward? How long and how hard will they work for a leader like that? It's easy to get wrapped up in our own perceptions and emotions and when under pressure, lack empathy, but if we emotionally react instead of empathetically respond, or we don't stop long enough to observe and question what someone else is going through, we set ourselves up to be

Leader 2. cared for the employee and for the immediate situation in life terms, not in work terms.

Empathy starts with caring about what others think or feel. Then, have patience and be still long enough to observe the thoughts and feelings of others and the various situations that are happening in other people's lives so that you can exercise more empathy. People come first. Yes, the business is critical, but nothing happens in business without people. Take *care* of the people and they will take care of the business. Always be empathetic.

"If you aren't humble, whatever empathy you claim is false and probably results from some arrogance or the desire to control. But true empathy is rooted in humility and the understanding that there are many people with as much to contribute in life as you." —Anand Mahindra

FOCUS ON STRATEGIC PLANNING AND EXPERT EXECUTION.

Too many leaders focus only on short-term goals, on winning the current battle, and are not focused enough on winning the longer war. This is particularly true when I speak to leaders with a military background. They make it very apparent why the United States of America's military has been so successful in battle. These leaders all spoke with a specific focus on winning *strategically*. Some told me war stories of being in a fire fight with the mission of stopping enemy advancement. They mentioned to reactionary leaders who instinctively gave only tactical orders such as deploying machine gunners to lay suppressive fire to keep the enemy from advancing, whereas the more seasoned leaders in advanced positions suggested strategic orders such as blowing up the only bridge available to the enemy. The origin on the word *strategy* can be traced back to Greek origins that means *the talk of Generals*. As a leader, are you looking for the proverbial "bridge" in your *war*, or you only always laying down "suppressive fire" from a machine gun to attempt to win a battle?

Even when you have a strategic plan, it is critical to execute the plan with precision and ensure that the tactics (and even the technology that supports the strategy) allow the strategy to be carried out safely and successfully.

WHEN THE STRATEGY ISN'T PROPERLY SUPPORTED, BAD THINGS CAN HAPPEN.

For years, I have had the privilege of being mentored by a thirteen-year military veteran, United States Army Special Forces Captain Robert (Bob) Wolfrom. I often consult with Bob on strategy and enjoy his examples of the importance of designing and deploying a smart strategy for all missions. Bob is always careful to point out that even with an intelligent strategy, the execution and tactics that support it are critical.

This was important to Bob because of his own experience, but perhaps more so because of his father's experience. When discussing strategy one day, Bob told me the story of his father, First Lieutenant Charles (Bud) Wolfrom, a U.S. Army Air Force Navigator on a B-17 bomber that flew in the mission on Schweinfurt–Regensburg on August 17, 1943, during World War II. The mission, intended to cripple the German aircraft industry, also was known as the double-strike mission or mission no. 84. In this strategic air raid, the United States sent hundreds of B-17 bomber planes to blow up factories that produced ball bearings and other mechanical parts for Germany's military.

Bud told Bob stories of the raid and noted that while the mission's strategic nature was valid and could have produced a huge advantage for the U.S. military, it was not executed as well as it could have been. Bud was one of only a few men from his squadron who even survived; fifty-five planes and five hundred and fifty-two crewmen were lost that day. Bud was one of about half of the lost crewmen who were taken prisoners of war and he was held for nearly two years. Most of the aircraft were lost over German-controlled land in Switzerland, or shot down at sea, with only five crews rescued. As many as seven airmen were killed and more than twenty were wounded aboard the bombers as they returned to base.

These losses were more than double the highest previous loss at that time. In addition, fifty-five to ninety-five planes were badly damaged during the mission. Couple that with hundreds of German civilian casualties and the fact that the mission was only a temporary setback for Germany, which was able to source parts from other parts of the country, and not many would consider the mission a success. In fact, the United States suspended all day-time raids after that mission.

Historians cite factors such as bad weather, which delayed the mission several times, and the fact that the bomber squadron wasn't accompanied by fighter planes, as primary reasons for such catastrophic losses, but I am convinced that there were hundreds of reasons why things turned out so poorly.

I am deeply moved by the sacrifice and wisdom of people like Bob and his heroic father, Bud Wolfrom. Bud completed the mission despite enemy fire that sent flak into his head and forced a crash landing in the icy English Channel, and his capture by German soldiers, who kept him as a prisoner of war for nearly two years. Despite all this, Bud, a Purple Heart recipient, lived to tell this story about the importance of many things, including endurance, bravery, and strategy, and ensuring that the right tactics and plans are in place to support any strategic mission.

A case in point is today's military battles. Heroic acts are performed daily and too many sacrifices are made to even mention here, and advancements in planning, intelligence, strategy, and technology, mean that missions like Bud's would be completed by a single, unmanned drone aircraft, with the ability to destroy threats thousands of miles away with a precision, laser-guided missile with little to no collateral damage, and then return safely back to base.

APPLICATION FOR THE THINGS THAT SCHOOL DIDN'T TEACH YOU

- Stay dedicated and persist. You must have the ability to endure the tough times.
- Focus on behavior over skill:
  - Integrity
  - Ability to inspire
  - Putting people first
  - Emotional intelligence
  - Communication

- You are what you consume, so consume wisely.
- Be naturally curious. Ask good questions and be determined to learn more.
- Encourage candor. Get to the bottom of things even if your feelings get hurt in the process.
- Focus on the quality of the questions you ask.
- Always respond; never react. Take the time to understand the situation before you offer your opinion or act. It is better to be delay a minute to decide than to take an hour to fix what was broken in haste.
- Actively listen. Don't focus only on your response; actively listen to others before formulating your response.
- Give your undivided attention to everyone. Great leaders are highly observant. It is nearly impossible to be truly observant when you are multi-tasking.
- Challenge the status quo. Remember, the seven most expensive words in business are "we have always done it that way."
- Rest strategically. You can only go so long at a fast pace before frustration and weariness show. As a leader, rest strategically so that you win long-term.
- Practice balance in everything. Know when to push yourself and your team and when to ease up. Everything in life is about balance.
- Be decisive. This doesn't mean to rush; it means that as the leader, it is your responsibility to get information, make decisions, and stick with them. If they are wrong, fix them and move on. Not every decision will be the best decision you have ever made.
- Use resources intelligently. Even if you have the right resources, ensure that they are readily available to your team and are used properly.
- Exercise and develop emotional intelligence, or "EQ." As leaders, we are in the people business. Make it a point to learn and grow your emotional intelligence and think about the human side of things first.
- Exercise empathy. Ask about people first. Ask what you can do and how the other person thinks and feels before giving your opinion. Act in their best interest first.
- Deploy strategy to focus on bigger picture wins that advance success. Just be sure that you have the tactics and support that will allow the strategy to be successful.

GUT CHECK 11: How much time are you willing to devote to developing the intangible, soft skills that matter most? If you know that these skills make the greatest impact, terrific—but how much time and energy, and how many other resources, are you willing to invest to develop them? If you don't, who will?

GIANT STEP TEN: STRATEGY PART 1- PEOPLE FIRST

It all comes down to people. Put them first.

"Be more 'intentional' on the people versus the mission. The mission and vision are a must; but people are forever." —Jack Plating

How far you see and reach as a leader depends entirely on the strength and height of the giants in your care. You must believe that in order to be a servant leader. And if you believe that, you must act on it every day. You must be willing and enthusiastic about putting people in the forefront of all that you do. Every decision, every investment, every change that you make—you must put people at the center. If a decision doesn't make sense for the people, it won't make sense for anything else in the long run—including profits.

Yeah, I said it: put people over profits. If you have made it this far in the book, you are not in business for the short term and you believe at least some of what I have included. Stay with me and don't stop trusting now.

When process or even profits are put above people, the rewards of profitability are limited, short lived, and typically incur huge, long-term expenses, including employee turnover and irreparable damage to the company's and leader's brand.

Yes, profit is the reason that businesses exist, but as we learned in the story of overusing fertilizer, when companies or leaders prioritize other things over people—even with good intentions to grow the business's market share or profitability—the results almost always backfire in a big way.

Leaders who refuse to put people above everything else miss the big picture. A team of properly inspired, developed, and driven people, all working towards the goal of profitability, will secure more profitability and success, and for many more years, than the companies that choose not to. Never underestimate people and their will to endure difficult things and ability to passionately help you and the business if they are inspired, developed, and believe how you believe.

Time + Proficiency x Purpose = Game-Changing Results

A FOCUS ON PEOPLE IS A FOCUS ON BUSINESS.

"When you get in critical situations in the game, don't think of plays, think of players."—Nick Saban

I learned the hard way that to be successful, I had to put people first, ignite passion, and take the time to truly know the people I counted on daily. As an assistant manager in the restaurant business in Houston in my early twenties, I was an expert in market statistics and trends, and facts and figures. I knew a lot about what should happen. The problem was, I didn't know anything about my most valuable resource: my people. Even though I had seen examples of how putting people first worked, I was young and dumb, still calling plays and not calling on players.

I focused so heavily on process and business and neglected to understand the restaurant's human resources; I did not even know some of my employee's full names.

Needless to say, I got my butt kicked for a couple of years. I did not run my restaurant; my restaurant ran me. To make matters worse, even with my intense focus on business, I could not get my food costs or labor numbers in line, no matter what I tried. I had tremendous employee turnover and felt about ten years older than I was.

Determined to turn things around, I invested in a ticket to see Zig Ziglar when he came to town. He said something that changed my thinking about business, my approach to employees, and ultimately the bottom line of the restaurant. This revelation continues to positively affect my life today. He said, "No one cares how much you know until they know how much you care . . . about them."

I consulted with successful restaurant leaders about this philosophy, and their message was clear. They succeeded because their people wanted to work—hard—for them. The leaders took care of the team and the team took care of the business. They understood their people; they knew their likes and dislikes. They knew the names of their people's children and even the sports teams they played for. These successful leaders had constructed a team of individuals determined not to let themselves or their leaders down. In short, they truly cared and put people first.

I started taking a sincere interest in the lives of my team. I made it a priority to know the things that were important to them and their families. I learned their likes and dislikes, making an effort to demonstrate my commitment to helping them feel like a part of something—a team, a family.

I ate lunch with them every day. I made it a point to cook and eat the dishes they liked to show respect for their various cultures and that I wanted to try new things.

I wanted to improve the way we communicated, so I invested every free minute to studying Spanish. The team was happy, because instead of playing the traditional radio stations as we prepared to open the restaurant, we listened to what the team wanted to listen to: Spanish radio. Taking the initiative to learn Spanish went a long way. Each member of my team went out of their way to assist me on this journey, and in turn, I helped them learn English.

I also let them work out minor schedule conflicts on their own. I even started a profit-sharing program with my head cooks and servers to encourage outstanding guest service and to tighten up food costs, giving them greater autonomy and sense of ownership. I created "potato captains" and gave my entire staff more autonomy and encouraged their feedback on important decisions made throughout the restaurant. Switching my focus to my team, and taking the appropriate actions, soon paid dividends.

The results were nothing short of amazing. We experienced a total turnaround of results and employee morale went through the roof. My restaurant guests were treated like royalty and guest return rates were higher than ever.

The positive energy literally transferred directly from my team to our guests. In addition, team morale and guest satisfaction were not the only things that improved; food costs and labor numbers improved to industry-leading levels and gross sales jumped an astounding twenty-seven percent year over year.

As a manager only focused on numbers and stats, I failed. As a leader, I built a team where we made a difference and created careers. I positively influenced my team through focus and care, and they positively affected me and our restaurant. Not a single person left the team through my promotion to general manager and over the following two years. I am not sure if that is some kind of record, but I can tell you that kind of tenure doesn't happen often in the restaurant business. And as great as the message from Zig was that day, I would argue that my decision and determination to change, and the actions that followed that decision, are what turned our results around.

IF YOU CARE, THEY WILL KNOW IT AND FOLLOW YOU ANYWHERE.

"I attract a crowd, not because I'm an extrovert or I'm over the top or I'm oozing with charisma. It's because I care."—Gary Vaynerchuk

Caring may be the most underrated business tool of all time. People will follow you when you care. This is not magic. If you really care for people and care about people, they will want to be around you and your company. They will fight hard and go to great lengths to ensure success. Are you concerned? Do you care? If so, how do you show it? Do you put people before process? Are you willing to express the care that you have to your team?

"People don't care how much you know, until they know how much you care . . . about them." —Zig Ziglar

THERE IS NO MODEL LIKE A ROLE MODEL!

"Your actions speak so loudly, I cannot hear what you are saying."
—Ralph Waldo Emerson

Model the behaviors you want to see, but never expect your team to be as committed, to work as hard, or to be as capable as you are. You don't pay them enough for that. If you want that kind of dedication, pay them like you are paid. If you do, give them stock in the company, as well. Otherwise, you can't expect the same things from them as should be expected from you. You should be willing to work harder and longer, and be more dedicated than anyone on your team. You can only properly build giants if you are giving them an example to work up to. You set the pace and model the behavior you want to see.

IT IS HARD TO MAKE BREAD WITHOUT ALL THE INGREDIENTS. HIRE WELL.

I am not saying that it is impossible to make bread without flour, yeast, salt, sugar, or water. What I am saying is that making bread is a hell of a lot easier if you use flour, yeast, salt, sugar, and water. If you fail to include yeast, your bread will not rise. If you don't use some kind of sugar, the yeast won't activate and your bread won't rise. In business, even if you have great plans, a fantastic culture, and a great product—most of the required ingredients—your company will not rise without *the right people.*

Hiring is the most important, yet most underdeveloped, skill of most leaders today, in my opinion. If you start with the right people, everything else can rise; without them, your business and your *bread* will inevitably fall flat.

"Human resources are like natural resources; they're often buried deep. You have to go looking for them, they're not just lying around on the surface. You have to create the circumstances where they show themselves."—Ken Robinson

MAKE BREAD THAT PEOPLE WILL EAT. HIRE DIVERSE TEAM MEMBERS.

What if no one can eat the bread you make? Yes, more of the bread analogy, but remember: bread is only *good* if the people eating it can tolerate flour, sugar, yeast, and so on. For years, people with gluten intolerance or other food allergies have altered the ingredients of bread so that they, too, can enjoy it. Besides, how boring would life be if there were only one kind of bread? Business is much the same. For years, studies have proven that leaders hire people who are like themselves. This inclination is at a subconscious level where a certain bias exists that causes us to hire safe choices who are as much like us as we can get. When we do this we simply bake the same bread over and over again, whether everyone can tolerate it or not. The worst part is, no one will ever tell you when the bread is bad.

We must be bold enough to step out of this natural inclination and hire diverse candidates who have different backgrounds and insights and push us to think and act differently. We cannot grow business or leadership by continuously baking the same bread for what will become a narrowing audience, and hope to be successful long-term.

To be clear, diversity isn't limited to a gender or race; diversity also means diversity of *thought*. Regardless of outer differences, the important thing is to hire and surround yourself with people who will be honest with you, who are driven and can positively contribute to your culture, and who believe how you believe.

One of the worst things that happens when you fail to hire a diverse team is that you lose candor. Workforces filled with "yes men and women" who agree with anything, at least to the leader's face, regardless of how they really think or feel, cause organizations to have slow or no growth, damaged brands, and shrinking profits.

This ass-kissing ritual cripples organizations by limiting growth to only as much as the person in charge can dream up or thinks is a good idea. It will simply be impossible for you to reach your full potential or your business to reach its full potential without people who will be honest with you when ideas are dumb, or when things are out of line, incorrectly prioritized, or not as they should be. Hire diverse.

RECRUIT, RECRUIT, RECRUIT.

"If you are looking for plants, don't discard seeds because they don't yet look like plants!" - Mikeal R. Morgan

I see so many leaders get arrogant when it comes to recruiting, as if the greatest candidates are lining up outside their door, begging for a spot. Companies that have a line of candidates typically have a line filled with inadequate candidates anyway. Most of the best-rated places to work make it a priority to recruit so they always have their pick of the best candidates. Depending the type of industry you serve, you should recruit pretty much everywhere. Even when I lead organizations that have specific requirements regarding education, experience, or skill sets, I am still recruiting for entry-level positions at restaurants, banks, or wherever I see passionate, talented individuals who I know could make a difference. Be a talent scout, willing to talk to people about what you do, how you believe, and the difference you believe they could make working with you. Most of the best people you could get to join your team are already happy somewhere else and not actively looking for a job.

HIRE FOR ATTITUDE OR SKILL? THE ANSWER IS *YES.*

The answer to the question of whether you should hire for attitude or skill is *yes.* The real question is, how you should prioritize? Ideally, you need both, but skill can be taught, and while I would argue that within the right culture, employees' attitudes can be shaped and molded, it's not too much to ask that a new employee bring a positive attitude and cultural fit when you onboard them. In fact, you should require this. When I say cultural fit, think of it not as *will* everyone get along, but rather, does this person *want to* get along.

AIM HIGHER AND FORGE AN EMPIRE.

"Don't hire people you can live with; hire people you can't live without!" —Jason Smith

Are you prepared to do battle, and would you go to battle with the group that now surrounds you? If you are trying to win, and win big, in business, you need to forge an empire, and that starts with the attitude and belief that you are indeed forging an empire. To have an empire, you must be surrounded by the best in the business. Therefore, you must be willing to set a high standard for recruiting and hiring. Take the time to put together a talent profile of the qualifications that really matter in a team member.

Don't require anything on the talent profile just because it has always been that way, or isn't something that you believe gives a person an edge. I know that my lack of formal education would have prevented me from filling many positions if the person hiring me had let it.

If a quality is needed and will help the person perform at a high level, it should be a standard. If it is something like an education standard, you should perhaps consider requiring the education or equivalent work experience. If you believe that the education is specialized and required for obtaining the best talent, on the other hand, then don't waiver. There are many jobs for which I know I wasn't hired because the hiring manager could not overlook the requirement for educational attainment, and I am okay with that.

KNOW HOW THEY REALLY ACT.

Have patience and build your list of the ideal candidates and do a great job of vetting the people even before the interview process. Meet in person first for coffee, tea, or lunch, if possible, in a casual setting. This lets you observe their behavior in a more natural setting. I worked for a company that taught us to recruit for executive leadership positions by using scenarios around an organized dinner, which allowed us to scrutinize and draw conclusions about candidates based on how they behaved.

For instance, in this case, how the candidate communicated with the server or other staff informed us about their communication skills with people other than us. This was often an indicator of how they are likely to treat subordinates or others within the organization. Similarly, some people think that a candidate who seasons food before tasting it might make decisions without first having all the information.

Other observations were slightly more contrived, like when we had it staged for the server to bring the wrong food out to see how the candidate reacted or responded. This was a great indicator of how they are likely to handle situations that don't go according to plan.

We didn't make any definitive decisions based on this one dinner, but the situation was helpful in gaining additional perspectives on how the candidate behaves and acts in settings outside of the office. Even if you aren't looking to take prospective candidates out to dinner, having a simple cup of coffee in a café with someone lets you observe and assess behaviors not typically displayed in an office setting.

PULL THE TRIGGER.

"The road is paved with squirrels that refused to make a decision."
—Anonymous

Be patient and do your due diligence when evaluating candidates, but when you know you have the right one, move swiftly to make an offer so that your hard work isn't for nothing and so you don't lose the candidate to another company in the meantime. Leadership is about making tough decisions, but when you do research and work the plan, you should have an easier time making them. Trust yourself and pull the trigger.

ALL ABOARD! YOU HAVE HIRED GREAT PEOPLE; NOW CREATE AN IDEAL ONBOARDING PROCESS.

Onboarding is one of the most overlooked processes at companies. As leaders, we are all either so "busy" in our day-to-day duties or we rely on another department like HR to onboard, that we often do not pay enough attention to ensure new staff are cared for in the way that creates a good and stable foundation.

I challenge you to review the onboarding process at your company. Examine every aspect of it and ask yourself whether, if you knew nothing about your company, it would answer your questions and give you a good feeling about the decision you just made to work there. When people are onboarded properly, they can better process the onslaught of new information and activities. It is hard enough to handle the complex systems, processes, and internal lingo of most companies when you have worked there for years, let alone when you see everything for the first time.

Onboarding should be fun and exciting, regardless of industries. Leaders should find new and exciting ways to begin creating culture warriors on day one. The more excited and educated your people are from the beginning, the better experience they are going to have and therefore, the better experience they will give back to your company. People want to feel welcomed. If you have done a good job recruiting and hiring, you should have people who believe how you believe and who want to learn how the company started, about its core beliefs and ideals and those of its founders, and how they could help realize those ideals.

The onboarding process should actually begin before the start date. The process should even include sending some type of care package of branded items, cups, pens, coffee mugs, and other items, and a handwritten note welcoming them. If this isn't available, how about a nice bouquet of flowers or a fruit basket—and yes, a handwritten note. The note should be written by the most senior leader of the new employee's department. Again, these investments build strong rapport and foundations for success early on.

On the first day of employment, new team members should be greeted by leadership, and welcomed into a clean, freshly stocked environment that is as personalized to them as it possibly can be. Don't take anything for granted. Show them everything from where the restroom is located and other logistics of the office surroundings, to where they can find a pencil if they need one.

Address every aspect of the job. Who are the other employees at the work location, and what do they do, and why? How do office politics work, and what are the various personalities in the work environment? If you are not in an office, personalize a bag for them and fill it with logoed items for the employee to take home. If possible, eat with the employee on the first day or have the team take the new hire out to lunch or sit with them at lunch time. Assign them someone to shadow for the first few days so that they can ask questions and get to know the office better. If this sounds like a lot for you to take on as a leader, it should! People first. That means that you must invest the time, energy, and effort from the beginning to forge an empire. This is built brick by brick via the people who are bought into your team, company, and program. If this seems trivial, stop and re-read this section. It is all about the details—the little things that most people think are inconsequential. That is what will separate you from others. Leaders who take the time and care enough to properly onboard will get a faster start and a more dedicated team member!

HIRED AND ONBOARDED—NOW WHAT?

Develop, develop, develop! Even if you hire the most experienced people you can find, they must be developed for your niche. Again, people are your greatest asset, investment, and foundation to success, and therefore, they must be constantly and consistently developed. If you have a standardized training program for new hires, re-evaluate it now. Go through the trainings and determine whether new hires get what they need to be successful. Does it sound like this would take a lot of time and energy? It will—and that is an investment great leaders make to ensure that their program is great. Most leaders will say the training or HR department is responsible for that, and that is fine. But who will ensure quality? Who is responsible for making certain that the training stays relevant and valuable? As a leader, you must ensure that all the work you did by placing the right people in the right jobs isn't undone by sub-par training.

Sub-par could mean many things. Is the new employee training conducive to learning? Are they exposed to the same or similar work challenges they will face once on the job, or are the trainings too simulated or theoretical? Are the trainings based on old methods that are no longer used in the field? Is the pace good? What media are used? Is there a mix of face-to-face, books, workbooks, writing, computer, or other methods so that all learner types are covered?

Once the initial trainings are completed, what is the ongoing development plan? How will you continue to grow your giants? How will you stimulate them intellectually and keep them challenged? When people are constantly challenged to learn new things or sharpen their skills, you create a growth culture where they feel it is not just possible to excel and grow, but also necessary, so don't wait to build the development plan. People also tend to stay at a place where they are planted and carefully grown.

(Insert shameless plug here!) If you need help designing or revamping a training and development program, don't feel like to have to do it alone; contact me and I will be happy to help! www.mikealmorgan.com

HIRED, ONBOARDED, AND TRAINED. DO I HAVE A GIANT YET?

Team members can't grow into giants until they are cared for. Many leaders become removed from the business the further up the ladder they go. They become exposed to things that the front line isn't exposed to and therefore develop a different perspective and understanding of the business. This is not a wrong understanding— or at least not every time—but one that typically is very different.

You must dedicate time to staying close to the field, so that you have both your understanding of the business as well as theirs. This multi-dimensional perspective helps you add value by knowing specifically how to care for your team. What tools do they need? What development do they need? What things will make their jobs easier, or at least simpler? You will only know these things if you are close to the team.

NOT MANY SHORT-STOPS THROW A HUNDRED-MILE-PER-HOUR FASTBALL. *PUT TALENT WHERE IT BELONGS.*

In the game of baseball, if a guy can throw a hundred-mile-per-hour fastball with extreme accuracy, not many coaches would make that guy the short stop. But in business, I have seen many instances of underutilized talent, or worse, people who are good employees and good at something but who are led to feel like failures because they are in the wrong job function. Pay close attention to the team and realize that outstanding employees can lag if they are in the wrong function. If they are a cultural fit, have a positive attitude, and could contribute to the business, try them in a different role before counting them out altogether.

MANY THINGS ARE EXPENDABLE, BUT GREAT PEOPLE ARE NOT.

Everything you do as a leader is easier if you have the right people. A great team will make the difference between your business being just okay or absolutely epic, so treat your team with this in mind. Typically, the most loyal, hard-working, and dedicated person at any business is the owner. The owner is typically the first one there and the last to leave and will work countless hours outside of "normal business hours." The business owner will go to great lengths to keep the business afloat, even mortgaging his or her own home.

Here is a secret: like in the potato captain scenario discussed earlier, a person who is treated more like a business owner will act more like one.

Don't let all of your hard work in recruiting, hiring, and developing great people be undone by not properly caring for them!

APPLICATION FOR PUTTING PEOPLE FIRST

- Surround yourself with people you can genuinely care about.

- Role model the behaviors you want to see.

- Focus on recruiting and hiring well. Hire for personhood over talent, as you can always develop skill.

- Surround yourself with diversity. You will never learn or grow, nor will your business, if you only surround yourself with people exactly like you. You must be willing to listen to opinions that differ from your own, as this will force you to think differently. Learn to surround yourself with and appreciate people who are different than you.

- Don't hire people you can live with; hire those you can't live without!

- Take special care when onboarding new team members. Make the onboarding process a special time that shows the spirit of your team's culture and sense of togetherness. Welcome new team members sincerely and invest the time upfront so they will stay invested in you and your company.

- People are not expendable. Never treat them as if they are.

GUT CHECK 12: People make the difference in this world. Whether it's a good difference or a bad difference is entirely up to how you lead and influence them. Surround yourself with people who believe how you believe, but don't reject them for thinking differently. Are you willing to be a long-term leader? If so, people must come before everything—yes, even including profits.

GIANT STEP ELEVEN: TRATEGY PART 2 –SIMPLIFY EVERYTHING

Simplicity enables speed and repeatable excellence

"That's been one of my mantras: focus and simplicity. Simple can be harder than complex: You have to work hard to get your thinking clean to make it simple. But it's worth it in the end because once you get there, you can move mountains."

—*Steve Jobs*

Most things are not simple, because simple does not mean easy. Have you ever implemented company policies that if followed, would work— yet no one followed them? Despite your best intentions, directions, policies, or processes that are complex are often not followed, even if doing so isn't *hard!* Simple and easy are not synonymous, so I am not advocating for you to not deal with things that are complex or hard. I am advocating for you to simplify the complex so that people understand what you mean and every aspect of the work can be done, regardless of level of difficulty.

It is hard to love what you don't understand. It is even harder to get other people to love, buy in to, follow, or use things they don't understand. Complexity is the root of so many business problems, yet most leaders either don't see it or refuse to believe it; do everyone a favor and don't be like them.

Just because you understand something very well, doesn't mean that anyone else will, and even when they do, they may not understand it to the extent you do. When this mismatch happens, people will disengage, and right or wrong, they will seek a simpler, often completely different alternative, such as not following the process you outlined at all.

Understand that I am not talking about skills, systems, or processes that seem complex only because the people being introduced to them are new to your industry's complexity. Everyone should understand that new things take time to learn and master. Instead, I am talking about the absurdity of how the simplest, most basic tasks can be made so complex.

If you simplify, you gain speed, and *good* speed is imperative to business growth, market share, and profitability.

A PERFECT PLACE TO EAT?

A few years ago, over the course of twelve months, I conducted a small, unofficial social experiment. Since we have so many out-of-town visitors to the office I work out of, I decided that every time someone asked me where they should eat, I would make the same recommendation in the same way and see how many would take me up on the recommendation. I would get very excited and very serious and first ask what kind of food they wanted. I then told them about the perfect place that sold the best (whatever they told me they wanted) at the best prices they had ever seen. I carefully explained that the only thing that came close to the great food was the friendly and attentive service.

This gave the visitors a personal, rave endorsement of the quality and value of my recommendation. I then let them know that the restaurant wasn't yet on the map, didn't have a website, and couldn't be found in GPS.

Here are the directions I gave:

"Proceed northwest for about one-half mile and then veer slightly east for about four blocks. When you see an old oak tree that looks like it's been struck by lightning, hang a right. But keep it slow because there is a driveway to the left about two hundred yards up

that road that you need to turn into. This driveway is just past the bushes where there is usually a big, black dog sleeping in front of. After you pass through the driveway, continue about two miles down the uptown road and turn left on right street. You will get about five blocks west of south street and you will see a sign that is red. That sign is for the blue bar. You will need to continue down the road for about three more minutes and take one more left at the red light. The place you want is going to be about another half a mile on the right. Just behind a business complex. You can't miss it."

Keep in mind that I was very serious as I gave these ridiculously complex directions so they could hear how simple the directions were . . . for me, at least.

How many people do you think took me up on my recommendation? None. If fact, most laughed or said, "Maybe that's not the place for me," or "We need somewhere we can actually find."

Again, simple doesn't mean easy, and it's been my experience that people are okay with that. Can you imagine if Dorothy in *The Wizard of Oz* got a series of complex directions? Dorothy already had to deal with a witch, flying monkeys, and other difficulties, but following the yellow brick road was *simple*, even though it wasn't easy. If you want people to find your "Oz," you'd better make it simple!

I'LL GOOGLE IT.

Most research data in 2019 show that anywhere between forty-six to eighty percent of the world's search engine traffic and as much as eighty-five percent of mobile search traffic flows through Google. But why is Google consistently the most-used search engine? Keep in mind that most of Google's users are not thinking about algorithms, feeds, rankings, metadata, or other technical terms, because they never have to. Google handles all of the complex stuff on the back end. Users never have to see the vast array of technological complexities that go in to making Google work so quickly and seamlessly. They use Google because they know that it loads fast, with the familiar, clean, and simple format that just works.

The page loads fast because there are no ads, no streaming videos, news, or other crap you are probably not interested in, anyway.

Google also offers plenty of free services for personal use like Gmail™, Google Docs™, Google Sheets ™, and Google Slides ™, to name a few. There are many reasons that Google remains the world's dominant search engine, but their claim to fame is really all about being simple and effective. Other than changing the Google logo to honor various holidays, artists, scientists, or pioneers, the main page has been the same since its inception, with a clean, white background and a blinking cursor already in the search bar, ready for you to type.

Just as people ask for a Kleenex™ instead of a tissue or a Band-Aid™ instead of a bandage, Google has redefined what it means to search so much so that it has become a verb: "I'll Google it."

Google is a prime example of a company that has gained mass popularity because of a simple, effective, user interface. They know that if it is simple and works, people will keep coming back.

I PHONE, YOU PHONE, NO PHONE LIKE IPHONE.

Things can be very complex but still be explained and used simply. In fact, the more complex things seem, the less people will want to use them. In 1985, Cray Research created the Cray-2 Supercomputer, which was water cooled and filled a small room. Today, according to technology experts, a single Apple iPhone 5 (nearly obsolete in 2019) has 2.7 times the processing power of the Cray-2 supercomputer and fits in the palm of your hand.

Apple is another company that has revolutionized an industry and turned the tech world on its side by releasing devices with unheard-of power, complex technology, and game-changing performance, all with a user interface that is so simple that a three-year-old can operate it.

Apple understands that a picture is worth a thousand words. Even when explaining the power and functionality of Apple products, Steve Jobs and other Apple leaders wouldn't use lengthy, text-heavy documents and graphs. They use presentations rich in graphics and simple terms and focus not on what the technology *is*, but rather, what it *does for you.*

You never hear Apple talk about how there are multiple "radios" and series of complex antennas inside of each iPhone. They simply explain how you can quickly and easily call people you love. People care less about details and more about benefits than ever before.

SELL ME THIS PEN.

When NASA first wanted to send astronauts into outer space, they sent them into simulations with ballpoint pens to write with. It was quickly discovered that a typical pen will not write in zero gravity or extreme heat or cold, upside down, or on surfaces such as glass, wood, metal, and so on.

At about the same time, a man named Paul Fisher invented a retractable, pressurized pen called the Anti-Gravity 7 (#AG7) that worked flawlessly in zero gravity. NASA bought this pen and placed it aboard the first manned Apollo mission in 1968. According to Fisher's website (www.spacepen.com), "Fisher's space pens are handcrafted and able to write underwater, over grease, at any angle, upside down, 3-times longer than the average pen, in extreme temperatures ranging from (-30°F to +250°F), and in zero gravity." That is impressive to say the least, and I am sure it is one of the finest writing instruments you can buy.

The Russians also went to space but never faced this dilemma because they went to space with a *pencil!*

Now, every time I get into a tough situation, I say to myself, my kids, or my team, "Use the pencil." Asking myself if there is a simple solution staring right at me pushes me to look for obvious answers before buying or creating one. It helps put things into perspective and simplify many complex situations.

I'LL HAVE A #1, PLEASE!

The fast food industry faces constant challenges, but years ago, it desperately looked for simple ways to improve two key parts of the business: selling highly profitable sides like French fries and sodas when people ordered items like hamburgers in a drive-through, and speeding up the drive-through process itself. For the first concern, they trained associates to sell customers on adding fries with catchy phrases like, "Would you like fries with that?" But implementing this took the associate convincingly, or at least consistently, asking every customer the question. It also added minutes to the transaction, which added to the second concern of speed. In many cases, the added time was not because of added costs, but rather because of the customer wrestling with the decision of how badly they should destroy their diet that day.

In response, the fast food industry developed the combination or "combo" meal. The combo meal groups an entrée and sides like French fries or other items, typically a drink and even a dessert in some cases, for a set price. Some combination meals group these items and discount them so it is cheaper than buying the items individually, making it a logical purchase.

When discounted, the restaurant will take a small hit on revenue but make up for it in volume and for selling items with a higher profit margin. The consumer wins even when the items are not discounted because of the simplicity of ordering, thus solving the restaurant's other concern of the need to move more people through the line faster, especially at busy times. Very few people visit the drive-through and order items one at a time, and instead preferring faster-moving lines, simple ordering processes, and more value (or at least more perceived value) thanks to the introduction of the combination meal. What is the proverbial combo meal of your industry or company, and can you simplify it enough to make it work well?

SAY WHAT? NEW ISN'T ALWAYS BETTER!

"The most successful businessman is the man who holds onto the old just as long as it is good and grubs the new just as soon as it is better."—Lee Iacocca

Communication is one of the things people most want to simplify, and for great reason. As I pointed out earlier, what's important is not what you communicate, but what gets communicated. When technology is introduced, however, people tend to over-complicate the means, methods, or delivery of communication. If you are looking to deliver clear, concise, and accurate information, do it in person any time you can. This way, factors like body language, tone, and expression are less likely to be lost or misunderstood. The next best thing is videoconferencing or video calling from a mobile phone. After that, voice calling is still a better alternative than texting. Furthermore, text and email communication are more widely used than in-person communication by ratios exceeding billions to one, which is all the more reason we should do everything we can to keep these forms of communication as simple and streamlined as possible.

A perfect example is the myriad different options for sending messages through social media via mobile phone applications. While all of them have some purpose, they all have limits. In most cases, both users must have the application installed and an active account to access the messages. And even when both users have access, some of these platforms have limitations such as the inability to send picture or video files, and so on. Using multiple methods often defeats the purpose of quick and effective communication.

I experienced this first-hand. A team I worked on used a group text message platform to get short messages and pictures to one another on a daily basis. A few guys on the team got excited about a new application that could send messages and wanted our entire team to start using it for our group communication instead of text. Our leaders agreed that we should try this new technology, so dozens of messages, along with several important updates, were blasted out to the group within the first few days. To our leader's dismay, some of the team wasn't following up or even replying to the messages. He found out that the people who weren't responding either didn't have the application downloaded, had issues with the account settings, or simply weren't seeing the messages because their notifications were turned off.

After we spent hours troubleshooting and training to ensure everyone was able to use the application, we noticed something: the app could not send picture messages, something our group often did.

When I took this to the guys who insisted we use this new technology, they said, "It's okay. When we need to send a picture, we can send it via the old text string and then send a message on this app to refer to the text for the picture."

This was maddening to me. These guys were so adamant about using something just because it was new that they overlooked the whole purpose of what we were trying to accomplish: to quickly and effectively communicate.

Using this new method cost us time, energy, and effort to load, learn, and use, and it couldn't even do everything we needed. But because it was new, these few guys thought it had to be better.

Innovation *can be* fantastic and is often how the world evolves, but newer is not always better; sometimes a "pencil" works just fine.

THE 3CS.

Teach your team a communication practice called the 3Cs and encourage them to use it. Always ask yourself, and have the team ask themselves, is the method, message, and the media Clear, Concise, and Complete? First, determine the best medium to convey the message. Will it most effectively do what I need it to do? Asking yourself questions like, will an email suffice, or should I call the person? If sending an email, do I need to send supporting documentation in the form of attachments or email strings? Will a text message work or does it need to be more formal? Next, move to the message itself. Is it a simple FYI, or is it a request for something? FYIs are straightforward, although I still believe that no email should be sent without sending at least a few words explaining why you have taken the time to forward it. When it comes to requests, if you can practice, teach, and reinforce the following few steps to your team, your entire organization can communicate more smoothly and efficiently.

Clear. Is my message clearly outlined? For example, if I am forwarding an email, am I simply forwarding a chain of emails and saying "see below" (if anything)? That is not clear. Clear would be slowing down to speed up and typing out exactly what is happening and what you need to happen, and then referencing the email chain to support or further explain your request.

Concise. Because people move so fast today and so much needs to be done in a day, ensure that your team understands how to condense their messages into as few words as possible, while still providing everything needed.

Complete. Do you give the recipient everything needed to fulfill your request? Does your message reference numbers, and other internally used figures that give the recipient additional information? Does it clearly, concisely, and completely outline *what is happening now and what needs to happen, while providing all data needed for them to act?*

Often when I teach this practice, I ask participants to ask themselves to act as if they were the recipient of the message that they are about to send, but that they knew absolutely nothing about the situation. Would they have enough information, clearly outlined, for them to take meaningful action? Have them walk you through how the person would read the message and then access all data needed. Usually, they must stop and add details that weren't originally in the message.

PLEASE FASTEN YOUR SAFETY BELT! SOPS: WHEN AND WHY WE NEED THEM.

With so much talk all through this program about giving people autonomy and freedom, not putting up fences, and so on, I want to be very clear in this section on creating *standard operating procedures*, or SOPs.

In any business, standards must be in place, rules followed, and people held accountable. You can do all of those things better if there is balance and you aren't governing people's thoughts or taking away their ability to have input on how things could be better, but also have clear, simple, standard operating procedures for processes or procedures that must be repeated to meet quality and/or safety standards. SOPs are good for anything that requires consistency, like a product or service, or needs to be duplicated in mass quantities with very few variants or errors. SOPs are also great for safety-related processes, such as the FAA regulations that all airlines have an SOP that stipulates how to hold a safety briefing. This is because before any U.S.-based flight is permitted to take off, the airline employees must conduct a safety briefing that covers emergency scenarios, no matter what.

Can you imagine if the FAA or airlines thought, "It's 2019, so everyone has surely flown before and knows that they should put the oxygen mask on if it drops from the ceiling, right?" Part of the SOP for the airlines, besides saying the same things on every flight, are visuals that show how to place the mask on your face or fasten your safety belt. These help the hearing impaired and more visual leaners so that many bases are covered, risks are mitigated, and safety is achieved.

SOPs should include:
- The SOP's purpose and why it's important
- The end goal of performing the SOP correctly
- How the outcome is measured
- Any tools or additional resources required
- Pictures, graphs, or other visuals
- Explanation of who is to perform each responsibility
- Outline of the operation in clear, step-by-step directions
- Date created and updated
- Contact person or department for suggestions

In clear terms the SOP should outline the expectation, the steps to achieve it, and any tools required. SOPs should include how the outcome will be measured or what success looks like. Many successful SOPs include graphics or other visuals that make it almost impossible for the reader to mess up.

When strong, simple SOPs are in place, you are likely to develop a team with a sharper skillset and less frustration about how to do certain things that are expected of them. You will also see improved overall performance, productivity and product quality, as well as consistency.

I once worked for a man who told us that if an SOP took up more than one half of one page, it was too long and probably too complex. While most of the SOPs we wrote couldn't be that succinct, we *were* able to keep them all to one page. He seemed pleased and later told me that one page was the goal all along, but he knew that if he'd told us to keep them to one page, we'd have more than likely used two.

GET FEEDBACK FROM THE FRONT LINE WHEN YOU BUILD SOPS.

Carefully observe the process to determine if something is missing altogether. Why are things in the process frequently not performed correctly? When you identify these issues, you can revise the SOP to address them and can even call them out so that the team knows that you recognize the challenges.

Provide the why behind the processes as well as the expected outcome, and the risks if the process is not performed correctly. This way, the team understands what is at stake and you get additional buy-in from them on completing the operation with care.

It's a good idea to include a date and contact paths, as well. This will serve a few purposes. You know when the SOP was last updated and whom to contact when the team does not get the expected outcome because of new or changed set of circumstances.

RAILROAD CROSSING, NO TRAVELING CARS

Listen when people give you suggestions. Here's an example of why this is important. My cousin worked for a railroad company for years and every day, he showed up to the rail yard and loaded, hooked up, and moved trains down the track to their destinations. The conductors and engineers who had been there for many years taught him how to do many things. He said that while the people who taught him did show him an SOP manual that covered everything you could think of that happened on the rail yard, most of the SOPs were outdated, inefficient, or even dangerous. One day, railroad leadership showed up to inspect things and ensure that people followed the SOPs. For the first several hours that passed, my cousin and his fellow team members followed every SOP to the letter—and not a single train left the yard.

The entire rail yard was gridlocked and hours behind schedule. The leaders were pissed off, to say the least, and called an impromptu meeting. When the senior foreman explained how the leaders shouldn't be upset—that the yard was simply following the SOPs—the leaders all changed their demeanor. How could there be such a disconnect? How did things get so out of hand that not one train could leave the yard when the SOPs were followed so perfectly?

The business literally was being strangled by its own policies. SOPs should be used, but they must fit the business model and the team using them, and be as simple as possible and updated to reflect changes in circumstances, people, climates, and so on.

GET SIMPLE. ASK THE GRANDMOTHER QUESTION.

"Okay, I definitely agree that simple it better," my client told me, "but how do I institute a culture that not only adopts, but prioritizes, simplicity?"

This client hired me to consult on ways to improve the company's online presence, specifically e-commerce and website utilization, after I explained that despite having good traffic, the website was difficult to navigate and had a poor user interface, which hurt sales and repeat business. He became frustrated as I informed him that the current website didn't even clearly explain what the company did to help people.

"Ask *the grandmother question*," I told him. "Ask yourself, if you had to explain the what, why, and how to your grandmother, so that she completely understood what you are talking about, could you?"

It doesn't matter that your grandmother isn't your target audience, and to be clear, it doesn't even matter if you understand it well enough to explain it to your grandmother; it only matters if you can *explain* it simply enough for your grandmother to understand it. For example, my grandma isn't a runner, (target audience) and neither am I, but I understand a marathon well enough to explain it to her. And while running a marathon isn't by any means easy, it can be pretty simply explained.

Me: "Grandma, do you know what a marathon is?"

Grandma: "No."

Me: "Well, it's a time-measured athletic event where you and many other runners run for 26.2 miles to see A. if you can complete it, and B. how fast you can complete it."

Ask this about every process you have—every computer system you use and application you install or website you publish.

Simple websites are more successful than those that aren't, period. After consulting with my client, we revamped his website so that what the company did for clients was clear. We used big, bold buttons that started the purchase process. The purchase button brought his clients to a wizard that walked the client through a series of questions that qualified them appropriately and even suggested appropriate add-on services. After a bit of marketing to showcase the new site's simplicity, website utilization went up fifty-four percent and online sales increased sixty-six percent. Customer reviews for his website improved from an average of 2 stars to 4.3 stars. His customers raved about the site's simplicity and how fast and easy it was to get products and services.

Ask the grandmother question about everything your company does and especially for every SOP you write. Don't limit it to technology related topics, either. Ask it about your current hiring and onboarding process, the training process, and so forth.

Most of the time, when you assess processes in terms of "could my grandmother understand this?" you will begin to understand how complex these things really are. This is important because when someone is new to your website or hired into your organization, they have about as much idea of what is going on as your grandmother does. When you simplify, you get immediate buy-in from employees and clients alike. People will not only be more inclined to try and use the things you offer, but they also will be more inclined to remember them and use them again and again.

You must set the pace at your organization (or at least on your team) so that everyone is encouraged to ask the grandmother question and will do everything possible to make and explain things in the simplest terms possible. Don't get discouraged when people don't understand things, but rather continue to simplify until the majority can understand them.

THE WORST PRACTICE

For nearly three thousand years, doctors used a procedure called bloodletting. This is where a person is strategically cut, and the body loses a significant amount of blood by simply letting it drip or drain out into a pan. How much blood depended on the symptoms and the doctor's experience and beliefs regarding the procedure and its effectiveness.

Some people theorize that bloodletting even contributed to the death of George Washington. In America, this barbaric practice was long ago replaced with antibiotics and other forms of significantly less invasive medicine and today is only used in very rare situations, by experienced physicians for very few conditions. But what if? What if people continued to perform bloodletting procedures, never trying to find breakthroughs in medicine, because that was the way it had been done for three thousand years?

Again, the seven most expensive words in business: "We have always done it that way."

So, how do you keep practices simple and good? How do you as a leader not fall into the trap of either keeping the status quo out of fear that nothing is better, and thus fail to innovate, or change too often just because something is new or because others are doing it, even if the results are not what's best for your team? Some of this could be rooted in the psychology of the words we use.

Here is the prime example. In most cases, the preferred way of doing something is called a "best practice." The concern with calling something a *best* practice, however, is that our brains instantly and subconsciously believe we should stop looking for anything better because we already have the "best" practice possible. The simple remedy is to start calling new methods "*better* practices." This way, beginning in our subconscious, we understand that it is probably not the very best way of doing things, but merely a better way. By only referring to them as *better* practices, our brains and our teams will remain open to looking at other, even better options, instead of being satisfied with the status quo.

A HAMMER POUNDS NAILS AND A WRENCH TURNS BOLTS: THE PROPER UTILIZATION OF RESOURCES

Using the correct resources is almost as important as using resources correctly.

As mentioned at least a few times before in this book, simple is better only if it is the right resource. Have you ever used a shoe to smash a bug or a screwdriver handle to bang on a nail? I know that typically when I use either of those seemingly simple fixes, I have mess to clean up on top of replacing whatever I broke in the process of using the wrong tool for the job. There isn't much difference in using the wrong tool or using the right tool the wrong way; you get a result, but it is rarely a quality one.

Many business teams are tasked with difficult work and when they do not use the tools and resources available, or they use them incorrectly, the work is inherently more difficult. This may sound oversimplified, but many leaders fail to ask themselves if they are properly using all the resources at their disposal. Moreover, leaders must be in the habit of examining how, and if, the team uses the proper resources and resources properly.

BUT WHERE IS THE TOOLBOX?

Tools must also be readily available or they will not be used. Availability is the primary reason that a shoe is the go-to weapon to attack a bug in the home, versus the bug spray that is inevitably locked in a cabinet, safely out of reach of small children.

I have seen websites, mobile technology, and other tools meant to help employees do their jobs better and faster go unused for years. When front-line employees are questioned, their answers are always the same: the resource is buried behind complex usernames and passwords, dozens of mouse clicks, or other actions that take substantially too long to access.

Worse, if you leave your team to source their own resources, you run the risk of them violating some type of safety, privacy, legal, or company regulation. For instance, I have seen teams create their own client-facing tools, when either none were provided, or the ones provided were too complex and the graphics for the documents created were sourced from various other proprietary websites. The company later faced copyright infringement lawsuits, all because the team didn't have the correct resources, or the resources were so complex that they were unusable. Should the employee have known better? Does all of the fault lie solely on the employee? Perhaps, but the company was the one responsible for paying the fines in the cases I am referencing. We as leaders ultimately bear the responsibility of ensuring that if the team needs a wrench, they can find and properly use the wrench designed for the job at hand.

FOCUS ON WHAT YOU CAN CONTROL!

You may have heard many times that you should "control the controllable," but what does that mean? It goes back to the results-oriented but change-focused paradox I introduced earlier in this book. When people work on what they can fully control, they work harder and with more purpose on that thing; the opposite happens when you ask them to control things over which they only have influence, but not the ultimate power to make something happen, or not.

When I speak to sales teams about this principle, I tell them that salespeople cannot control whether a client will buy their product, but they can control how many clients they have in the pipeline to sell to. They can control their outbound sales efforts, follow-up activities, and attitude. These things, well controlled, will yield the desired sales outcomes.

So, what about your industry? What should your team remain focused on? Because people tend to only focus on what is easy—like pointing out what can't be done or what isn't available—as a leader, you must keep people grounded and focused on what they can control. Here are my top twenty factors that I can control. How many more can you add to your list?

Things that I can control:

- My attitude
- My level of gratitude
- How often I say *please*
- What time I wake up
- Whether I respond or react to situations
- How hard I work
- Whom I follow on social media
- What I eat
- What I listen to
- What I believe
- How I treat my body
- What and how often I read
- How many random acts of kindness I perform
- How I spend my money
- Whom I spend time with
- What I say *no* to
- Not quitting when things are difficult
- How honest I am
- Whether I ask for help
- How often I leave my comfort zone

A great exercise to reinforce the things you and the team should stay focused on is to have each member come up with their own list of controllable items, then share with the team. Delete duplicate answers and use the remaining list as the minimum expectations for the team. If people are intensely focused on all of the things they can control, the results they produce are almost always more favorable. This exercise will help simplify things and helps the team feel less overwhelmed by identifying and focusing on only the things they can control.

HOW DO YOU SIMPLIFY THE MESSAGE? THE TRIAD CONCEPT ™

How do you make the complex, simple? How do you get a message or process simple enough so that people remember and use it? Since it is proven that people are more likely to remember things when they are presented in threes, I use what I call the triad method.

It is simply a process that highlights the highest level of whatever it is I am trying to get to. Doing this simplifies the message, making it easier to effectively use, communicate, and remember. It also gives some autonomy to the people using it because these are more like high-level concepts or goals of the overall strategy, and people can be inventive in order to achieve them.

It can be used in any industry or for anything, really. For instance, when the technology my team sold became increasingly complex, I knew I needed a simple, repeatable sales process that my team could learn, remember, and use. I also wanted something that my managers could use in coaching and improving sales.

Like a traditional brainstorming session, I begin by thinking of all the things that are important in the process. I make long lists of everything important. I then separate the lists into high-level categories, putting similar things together and eliminating duplicates.

At this stage, you should go for quantity and there should be many lists. The goal is to continue to consolidate the lists until you have the highest level of topic or the most important action word(s) you can find. Form three lists of your top actionable items that best support the objective. Each of the three lists should support one of the most critical aspects of the objective. Keep the strategy to only three key things and continue to consolidate the list of verbs and choose a key word to lead each of the three parts of the strategy. The other ideas are executable tactics that support the strategy.

I use another trick to boil the lists down into action words, a method called "if I want, I should." The process looks like this: "If I want (insert word here), I should (insert the word you must do to achieve the first word here)." So, if I come up with an important quality for salesperson to focus on, such as being smart, then I simply say, "If I want to be SMART, I should REASERCH, STUDY, or LEARN."

In sales, people buy from people they like, so I crafted a sales strategy that had a long list of qualities that fed the main idea, or leg of the strategy of being liked. I knew that I needed the highest level of action that supported someone in being liked, so I titled the category "Be Nice." All other things in this list served as supporting tactics.

I also knew that people buy from people whom they feel add value, so I had a long list of all the things that salespeople should do to add value to clients. I titled that list "Add Value." And finally, I knew that one of the biggest reasons that salespeople fail is the lack of meaningful follow up, so the last list was titled "Follow Up." Again, the lists under these main titles were long and served as tactics that allowed the sales teams to execute the main strategy in their own way or to pursue the other tactics in the list to support their overall strategy.

If you are nice, people will want to do business with you.

If you add value, people will feel compelled to do business with you.

If you follow up correctly, people will consistently do business with you.

Writing a sixteen-point strategy with subchapters and details is easy. Getting your ideas so distilled and concise that they can be articulated in three points is challenging, but rewarding. So, before you knock this exercise of brainstorming and coming up with a three-point strategy, I challenge you to try it so you can see first-hand just how difficult simplifying can be. Keep in mind that *simple* isn't by any means *easy* to accomplish.

Take the sales philosophy that I came up with as an example. Being nice is hard enough for some folks, even on a surface level. And even the nicest people find it challenging to up their game each day with everyone they come into contact with.

And as for adding value, entire books have been written regarding how to add specific value to prospects and clients, so this point may be the most difficult of the three, if done very well.

Following up correctly is one of the most overlooked tactics in sales. Most people do not know how to follow up correctly because they either fail to ask their client what correct follow up means to them or they fail to correctly execute on what their client told them.

The point is, while this is only a simple, three-point sales strategy, it works! That's because salespeople remember it and can actually execute on it. It's also because leaders can coach, develop, and challenge teams based on these three pillars, enabling a consistent, challenging, and overarching message. And finally, because it prompts people to think and be creative while working towards the objective. How can you take your priorities and simplify them using this Triad Method?

"Truth is ever to be found in simplicity, and not in the multiplicity and confusion of things." —Isaac Newton

CREATE A CULTURE OF SIMPLIFICATION.

All great leaders look for ways to simplify processes to make their team's jobs easier. The question is, how much can you alone see and impact? How can you touch every process in every part of your business? It isn't enough for you to just simplify matters; you must make simplification part of your culture so that everyone seeks ways to make things simpler. Smart companies, depending on their size, dedicate many resources and even entire teams to gathering and implementing employee ideas for simplification. Even these processes must be monitored, though. I have seen first-hand a case in which the team responsible for making these changes created confusion and did more to push back than to implement new and better ideas.

In the end, it may be nearly impossible for you to touch every complex process, system, or concern at your company, but it is possible for you as a

leader to develop a culture of simplicity, where everyone is responsible for ensuring simplicity in everything they touch. Everyone must be taught that if something is perceived by even a small group of people as being too complex, the entire team should support change, and then work to simplify it.

SIMPLIFICATION NEVER ENDS.

Think of simplifying everything like painting a ship that stays out at sea. The second you finish, the place where you started is damaged in some way and you must turn around and start all over again. Your business cannot be too simple. Simplification only makes dealing with the complex things easier, better, and faster.

APPLICATION FOR SIMPLIFY EVERYTHING

- Simplification helps keep people happy and helpful. It also equals speed and efficiency. It is not important—it is absolutely paramount!
- Clarify and create a plan around the three C's for your communication. Ensure that everything you and your team is doing is **clear, concise,** and **complete!**
- Create good, simple SOPs using input from the team and that are easy to follow and update.
- Learn to make and keep things simple by asking the "Grandmother Question."
- Never refer to anything as a "best practice." They are only "better practices." Be determined to continuously look for better ways of doing things.
- Use resources correctly and look for better ways to improve resources, always ensuring that all resources are available to the team.
- Control the controllable. Put a plan together and hold people accountable to the behavioral aspects of the business. This will grow your culture and your business.
- Create a Triad Concept for the things that you need to simplify, highlight, or communicate.
- Create a culture of simplification that teaches the team to value simplification. When the entire team looks for ways to simplify everything, everyone wins.

GUT CHECK 13: People will do what they understand and believe in. It is your job as a leader to simplify anything that is complex, even if you don't believe it to be complex. Simplification can take time, be tedious, and require the input of others to be most effective. Will you commit to taking the time, energy, and effort required to simplify your business?

GIANT STEP TWELVE: STRATEGY PART 3 – INSPIRE EVERYONE

How to be a handwritten note in a world full of emails

"I've learned that people will forget what you said, people will forget what you did, but people will never forget how you made them feel."

—Maya Angelou

A s a human being, you have the opportunity to positively impact people's lives; as a leader, you have the obligation to do so. And "inspire everyone" means *everyone*. Every team member, client, family member, or stranger you encounter on the street. Sound exhausting? It is extremely exhausting! I could go on about how it should be energizing and inspiring—and it should be—but if you do it right, it is also exhausting! Completely, drop down and collapse, exhausting!

In sports, there are few things more disappointing than watching a runner end a race and still have energy and stamina. When a race is over, the runner should have left everything they have out on that track. They should have nothing left, not even the ability to stand. If you want to see a fine example of this, watch the grainy, gritty film from the 1954 race dubbed the miracle mile, between Roger Banister and John Landy. This was the first race recorded where two runners ran a sub-four-minute mile. At the end, the winner, Roger Bannister, collapsed in the arms of his trainers, proving he left all he had out there.

Leaders should show this same level of intensity as we run the race of leadership every day! The title of this chapter and part of the leadership strategy is not called *motivate* everyone, because inspiration and motivation are different. Motivation is good and every leader should motivate the team to *action*, but inspiration is a deeper, permanent *feeling* that invokes thought and drives meaningful action.

There is something to be said for taking your time and making people feel special, wanted, and encouraged. It is a skill that is required for leadership excellence. But, like many of the other traits and skills listed in the previous chapters, positive, personal impact is unfortunately not taught in any classroom. Your team's positive, personal impact should be decided on a person-by-person basis, as everyone is unique and special and touched by different things. It is in this that you will build a culture of excellence that few will leave, and many will fight to join.

BUT DOESN'T IT TAKE TIME TO INSPIRE? SLOW DOWN TO SPEED UP!

"The hurrier I go, the behinder I get!" —*Lewis Carroll's White Rabbit from Alice's Adventures in Wonderland*

When many people think of speed, they think of the cheetah, which can reach speeds of seventy miles an hour in short bursts. But if you examine a cheetah's behaviors, you will see that it is its ability to be slow and calculated that makes it the world's fastest land animal. First, the cheetah is only fast when it absolutely must be. It exerts maximum energy only after it has carefully identified and analyzed its prey, the landscape, other predators, and every other relevant factor. The cheetah conserves energy and rests strategically, hunting only the right prey at the right time, in the right conditions. It knows that it only has so much energy for so long and that the effort must result in a win, or it can't eat—another example of the secret formula at work (*Time + Proficiency x Purpose = Game-Changing Results*).

There is a great deal of video footage of cheetahs analyzing prey without acting, even when the prey is close, weak, or seems to be highly vulnerable, because it knows and sees things that we cannot due to its vantage point, outside influences, or calculations of conditions. In other words, more important than the cheetah's ability to be fast, is the wherewithal to slow down so that it *can* speed up if needed.

And while it may seem counterintuitive in business to slow down in order to speed up, it is a concept that underlies several other topics in this book, such as written communications, strategically resting as a leader, and a few others. Inspiring everyone means first being conscious of everyone and everything.

It means being fully aware of the people around you, and what role they actually play and what moves them. Not just knowing surface-level things, but the deep, emotional things, to the extent possible. It is the ability to analyze people, your surroundings, and external conditions and strategically act when it matters most.

The first time I saw a leader really slow down and take the time to inspire, I was sixteen years old and working as a dishwasher in the dietary department of a hospital. The hospital administrators, executive leaders, and even several surgeons periodically toured the hospital, and about once a year, they came through the back part of the department where my co-worker and I spent our time. In tow was always a herd of lower-level managers, busy asking questions, directing the others about, and rushing them from one place to another.

Because of this, the leadership never stayed in one department for very long on these little tours. One day, however, the head of the hospital system struck up a conversation with me and one of my coworkers. He asked us about what we did, how long we had worked there, what we enjoyed most about the work, and so on. He also asked about our families, where we lived, and what we did for fun. We shared some details and he shared some about his family and where he grew up, as well.

After twenty minutes or so, as we talked while the rest of the group stood there, the man looked up and with a firm voice, said to the others, "Carry on, I'll catch up in a bit. This is important." The group looked a little puzzled but kept moving as we continued. As we wrapped up, before the leader moved on, he told my coworker and me how valuable we were and how important our work was. He told us that no one at the hospital eats if there are no clean dishes and that we should take pride in being the "backbone of the entire hospital system."

After the leader moved on, my coworker turned to me and said; "I've never felt so important here as I do right now. He didn't have to stop and talk to us, but he did. He cared and it showed."

This was more than motivating to us; it was inspiring. The sense of pride and value he instilled in us lasted the entire time we worked there. We saw the leader in passing from time to time and he always made time to check on us, shake hands, and ask about family. He made his primary impact and then periodically invested a few minutes here and there to keep it going.

As I reflect on that event, I am even more impressed by the fact that the leader took twenty-five minutes or so out of his day and made us a priority. That twenty-five minutes wasn't lost; it was invested in his people. And the return on that investment was a few people that from that point on, had higher productivity, didn't want to miss a day of work, and produced better work because of a sense of pride and value. More than a year later, my coworker and I still took particular care cleaning up as we left for the night, mopping the floor and re-wiping equipment to a high shine. One of the more disgruntled cooks walked by and asked why we cared so much. We looked at each other with a smile, and in unison said, "You never know who may walk through here."

This leader knew the value of slowing down to speed up. People are worth your investment. Don't let the pressure of budgets, deadlines, or anything else deter you from investing time in the most important asset you have—your people!

INSPIRATION STARTS WITH A MOVEMENT TO INSPIRE!

Your leadership brand must be this: once people see what you do for others, they want to rally behind you and support your work, much like in a political campaign. The difference is that your work must be continual, genuine, and not for the purpose of gaining a title or office, but rather solely to support, serve, inspire, and lead others.

As I previously stated, *people like to love, but they love to hate.* You must work hard to inspire. When people see a positive movement, they want to be part of it. It is contagious. You won't even need to invite people to follow you as the leader; you just need to *help yourself* by staying focused on the movement, and not worrying about how big or fast it is growing. Your job is to manage its impact on everyone involved.

When people see someone helping themselves even when they need more help, they are innately encouraged to join in. A great example is when you see someone's car stalled on the side of the road. When I see a stalled car with the person just sitting there, doing nothing, I notice that no one pulls over to help.

On the other hand, when the stranded motorist gets out and starts to push the car, (even if the person knows it is impossible to move a heavy vehicle by themselves), others stop to help. People want to be a part of—and contribute to—something that is good. As a leader, you just have to be willing to get out and push first.

CREATE AN INSPIRATIONAL VISION SO BIG, IT SCARES YOU!

"Leadership is the capacity to translate vision into reality."

—Warren Bennis

It is easy to motivate but nearly impossible to inspire if you don't have a vision that moves people. Leaders who effectively build giants have far-reaching vision statements that don't just push boundaries, but that put butterflies in people's stomachs! Not a goal, not a plan, a vision is something big and audacious that moves you to big actions. Your vision should be so bold that you second-guess it when you think about it. It should scare you when you write it down and it should totally freak you out the first time you share it with others. If your vision isn't big enough that it scares you when you first think about it, it isn't nearly big enough! When a vision is big enough that it scares you, it energizes you to think differently—to do and be more! *Scary* visions are the ones that start movements that change the world.

But before you can surround yourself with people who believe how you believe, follow your vision and launch a movement, you first must be able to articulate your vision.

YOUR VISION IS NOT WHAT YOU COMMUNICATE— IT'S WHAT GETS COMMUNICATED!

A vision statement is a single, flowing narrative made of three parts:
1. The Proclamation of the Vision (including results and timeframe)
2. Quantifiers (tangible or measurable aspects that allow you to define and quantify milestones and accomplishments)
3. The Human Element (the vision's connection to others, the end results, or overall benefit to others)

The proclamation is what you, you and the team, or the company will achieve. It should be a goal that is precise and measurable, has a timeline or time frame, and describes what the end result looks like.

On May 25, 1961, President John F. Kennedy proclaimed his bold vision that the United States would put a man on the moon and safely return him by the end of the decade. Can you imagine what the people closest to him must have thought? The idea was certainly bold—and even scary. *Side note: How cool is it, that as bold and scary as that vision was to some, on July 20, 1969, Neil Armstrong did indeed step foot on the moon and then safely returned?*

Quantifiers state how you will measure achievement and are included in the proclamation itself, like in the case of JFK's vision to put a man on the moon. A *man* being *on the moon*, by the *end of the decade* and *safely return*, were the quantifiers.

Finally, **the human element** adds a relatable touch that connects people personally with your vision! If people can't connect with what you want to achieve—if it doesn't matter to them or doesn't change anything—they are less likely to support it or work for it. Think in terms of end result or benefit to others. What's in it for them—why should they care? How will accomplishing this vision change anything?

JFK regularly talked about how, as a country, we needed to lead the world in technology and innovation—and what better way to prove it than being the first people to put a man on the moon?

You have seen politicians do this for years, promoting a large-scale vision that is for one thing with the end-result (or in some cases, the by-product) for the people, such as better education, safer communities, or other issues that touch people's hearts. Then, when it comes to working for it, campaigning on its behalf, or even raising taxes to achieve it, people are not only behind the movement and higher taxes, but actively vote and campaign for its implementation.

Be bold when you set a vision and make sure that it scares you. And it is okay to have it so bold that it may not be accomplished in a decade.

Microsoft proclaimed a vision of putting a computer on every desktop, in every home. Some would argue that they have accomplished this, but even if you disagree, they have at least come very close to fulfilling their vision *and* that their vision helped drive them to become as big and successful as they are today. In the 1880s, the vision of George Eastman (the founder of Kodak), was to make photography as simple as using a pencil. Most would agree, that he, along with the employees at the Kodak company, in fact fulfilled that vision.

TELL THEM HOW FAR THEY HAVE ALREADY COME. COMMUNICATE MILESTONES.

I can tell you that when leaders proclaim bold visions, it can be make you feel a little weird and even a little frustrated when you first hear it. I can specifically remember hearing leaders announce their visions and looking around the room only to see the crowd's collective eye rolling, smirks and other signs that they were thinking to themselves, *Yeah right, like that's ever going to happen!* But then a few months later, the leader stood up in front of the crowd and announced that a small milestone had been met—they were well on their way to making the vision real! It is important to communicate and even celebrate small milestones. People need to feel that they are making progress to stay focused and motivated.

Figure out what needs to be done and who you need behind it, then take small steps. Measure and communicate milestones and build on this momentum and excitement as you talk about what working toward the vision means to the people behind it. This will start a movement of sorts and have more and more people standing by you, fighting for the vision and contributing in their own unique way! Be sure that you are not just celebrating "lag measure" milestones, such as tangible achievements, but to also behavioral and other intangible or "lead measure" milestones that also position you for success. These could be things like activities or actions that if done well, will lead toward the vison. Keep in mind that farmers must first "lead measure" things like how many seeds to plant, soil conditions, water consumption, hours of sunlight, and many other factors before they can "lag measure" the harvested crop weight.

Take comfort in knowing that by accomplishing all of these milestones, you will eventually accomplish the tangible fruits of your vision. And while you should set a reasonable timeframe, in the spirit of keeping the vison big and scary, *it is better to expand the timeline than to reduce the vision!*

GO TO THE PLAY, OR I'LL FIRE YOU. INSPIRATION THROUGH TRUST.

"Without trust we don't truly collaborate; we coordinate or at best, cooperate. It is trust that transforms a group of people into a team." —Stephen Covey

For years in my career as a sales manager, I was blessed to be led by a great man named Thomas (Tem) McHugh. From the very beginning, I could certainly tell that he put people first and trusted his team. After only a few months of working with Tem, I faced a dilemma that proved how seriously he took these principles.

My daughter had a school play that I wanted to attend but it happened to be right in the middle of the day. While we weren't bound to a desk, this would be time out of the field, and I wasn't sure how strict he would be about this time being taken for a non-work-related activity. As I debated whether I should even mention where I would be for that hour, he happened to call.

My integrity instantly spurred me to inform him of my intentions to go to my daughter's play—with his permission, of course. He paused for what seemed like ten minutes and then said, "Listen very closely, Mike. If you don't attend that play, I'll fire you!"

I said, "I beg your pardon?"

He said, "I'm not really going to fire you, but I needed to get your attention."

What he said next meant everything to me: "Mike, ten years from now, no one will ask you about how many sales you made this month, or even where you worked, but your daughter will remember very vividly if you do or do not attend that play!"

He went on to explain that while work and taking care of business is critical, we must have priorities and balance. He may not have realized it at the time, but that single act of trust and leadership moved and *inspired* me to do more and be more. This inspiration compelled me to work harder and do as much as possible for my family, my clients, Tem, the team, and the company.

What Tem figured out—that many never do—is that trust helps employees understand that they can succeed both in their jobs and with their families. He taught me that these types of actions, when taken by leadership with the right people, are not only critical for a team's personal and professional growth, but that they also inspire and move individuals to do and be more.

THE BALANCE OF FEAR IN LEADERSHIP: FEAR SHOULD ONLY BE AN INNOCENT BYPRODUCT OF ACCOUNTABILITY.

Every relationship, both personal and business, should be based on love, or at least great intention if only at the human level, but there also must be some level of fear in every relationship for it to be successful long-term. This is true even in a marriage. And sometimes fear keeps people more honest than love will alone. For instance, if one person contemplates being unfaithful in a marriage, even if they are in love with their spouse, the fear of being abandoned by their spouse is enough to keep them faithful. Fear is what keeps temptation in check. Many people choose not to engage in criminal activity not because they are so good, but because they are afraid of being caught and held accountable. A relationship entirely based on fear, however, can be successful only in the short term, if at all.

You are the leader—there is no need to yell and scream, be an asshole, or walk around instilling fear in all those you are supposed to serve. Fear emerges naturally because it is a byproduct of accountability. Fear is present even in cases of the most loving, caring, and even introverted leaders, because of accountability.

If you have hired well, developed and cared for your people, outlined your expectations clearly, shared your leadership philosophy, and communicated clear goals, and if you have provided simple and ample resources, you should hold people accountable to a high standard.

This goes back to the adage of, *"You should strive to be great to work for, not easy to work for."*

The important thing is the intent behind accountability and the manner in which accountability is enforced. If you enforce accountability measures solely to instill fear, you are an asshole abusing your authority. Holding people accountable due to poor performance or behavior, and responding in a way that is meant to help, with pure intent, is helpful to both parties and establishes accountability.

I put many people I served through the years on some type of performance program, or other form of disciplinary write-up, either formally or informally, when warranted. I did this not to intimidate or terminate them—in fact, quite the opposite. I needed them to understand that while actions—or lack thereof—have consequences, there is also a plan to improve their behavior or performance.

I also needed them to understand that their way wasn't working, and that change was needed. This reinforced that even if they didn't agree with the outline of my plan, they needed to adopt *a* plan and change their results.

As a leader, you need your team to understand that we must all be held accountable, since that is what keeps us true, but we can do so in a way that keeps our dignity and even our pride intact.

TO INSPIRE THE HEART, STIMULATE THE MIND.

One of the best ways to touch people's hearts and inspire them is by stimulating their minds. But how much of your time is spent purposely getting people to truly, deeply, think? My research and experience have shown me time and time again that people are inspired more when they are forced to think than when they are simply given some profound piece of wisdom that merely informs. Therefore, the process of intellectual stimulation is easier reached through providing information *and* asking questions than through offering information alone.

Just getting a person to think about the details of a topic or situation in some instances is enough to stimulate and begin inspiring them. For the basic details, the basic questions of what, when, and how will uncover details when asked in the sincerest manner possible. Sincerity ensures that your questions don't come across as an interrogation, but rather, sincere curiosity.

Share something with a person and ask questions like, "How could you see yourself using that?" Or, "When you think of this topic, who does it make you think about?" Or, "Who is the first person you would share this with?"

Think about the people who, when you are around them, push you to be better, to grow, and to move past obstacles—the people who truly inspire you. These are the ones who typically do a good job of stimulating you intellectually. And this usually comes from the quality of questions they ask. More specifically, it comes when they sincerely and genuinely ask you *why*. Getting people to understand *why* they think or feel a certain way about a particular topic prompts them to think at a deeper level. This leads to them thinking about why it is truly important to them and therefore taps into their inner purpose or heart.

This is also effective because people are inspired when they are listened to and when someone takes the time to understand what is important to them.

Spend time developing the skills of asking deep, probing questions that stimulate people's minds, and through that you will be better at inspiring their hearts!

THE SIMPLE THINGS THAT REALLY MAKES THE DIFFERENCE, FEW WILL DO.

"When I talk to managers, I get the feeling that they are important. When I talk to leaders, I get the feeling that I am important."
—Alexander Den Heijer

If you focus, pay attention, and invest in the people in your organization, you can take simple steps that will impact them. For instance, I—like you, I'm sure—have had many work and wedding anniversaries, birthdays, and other life milestones that went unnoticed and unrecognized by many, if not all, of the leaders in my organization at points in my career. And while this is more common in large organizations, this certainly should not be the case. Regardless of the organization's size, leaders should take the time to recognize the meaningful events in their team's lives. That said, this is basic stuff, which to me is in fact the table-stakes in every organization—or at least, should be. This is "low-hanging fruit" when it comes to ways to inspire people. Invest the time and find out when the important dates are in your team's lives and be sure to recognize them. It matters!

HOW DO YOU REALLY MAKE PEOPLE FEEL SPECIAL? IN A WORD, SERVE!

There are so many ways to serve your team and show them you care. One minute of personal connection or one simple act is worth so much to our people. How many times have you taken the time to have a cup of coffee with someone on your team? Moreover, how about someone two, three, or more levels below you in your organization?

The goal is to express a small act of servitude that will not only touch people on an emotional level, but that are contagious. When you lead, others follow; when you care enough to serve, people will follow you anywhere.

WHEN IT RAINS, YOU CAN SHINE!

At various time, I have stashed golf umbrellas at the office, and when it rained, I would grab a few and escort team members and others who worked in the building (who didn't even work for the same company I did) out to their cars so they didn't get wet. Why did I grab multiple umbrellas? Because when people saw me, they wanted to do the same. We created a real experience of servitude that people felt good about and remembered.

Several months after one of these umbrella walks, a team member approached me and told me how grateful he was for the act of kindness. Then he said something that inspired me: "That day made me want to follow you, rain or shine!"

IT WAS GAME ON, WHEN THE GAME WAS ON.

If there is a sports game on TV that is important to your team, instead of creating rules around *not* watching it, do what I have seen other leaders do: host office watch parties. Bring projectors or televisions into your board room and personally serve popcorn or other snacks while the team watches the game. One such game was near a deadline for a very important project, and when the team asked our leader if that changed anything, she simply said, "Hell no, we are watching it for sure! This game is only being played *live* this one time, ever."

After the game, the entire team stayed and finished the work. We experienced incredible levels of teamwork, with laughing and great fellowship, and within a few hours, we made such strides that we finished the project prior to the deadline. It's okay to have a bit of fun and in that act of prioritizing people, a bit of inspiration floats out and finds its way into people's hearts.

HAND-WRITE YOUR WAY INTO THEIR HEARTS

It takes time, energy, and effort to inspire others and because of that, many people will simply not follow through. But even small things, when carried out with genuine intent, will have a powerful, profound impact. A few dollars spent on stationery and stamps, coupled with a few minutes to write an inspiring note and mail it to someone, is a game changer. I am not sure what it is about a handwritten card. Maybe it's the nostalgia of getting a card with money enclosed from a relative when we were kids and reliving that excitement. Or perhaps just the fact that handwritten notes are increasingly rare as most everything that comes in the mail these days is bills.

We live in a world overrun by technology and rarely take the time to exercise the art of handwritten communication. Studies show that most people will actually open a hand-addressed envelope while still at the mailbox but wait to open the rest of the mail until they are inside.

If you want to take this to the next level, let me share an even *better practice* with you. I shameless stole this from an extraordinary leader who I am lucky enough to call my friend and mutual mentor: Mr. Jimmy Ables. The ironic thing about Jimmy is that he is brilliant when it comes to all things advanced, digital, and technology related, but perhaps his real brilliance is how he is able to use very basic, analog methods to lead and inspire—things like listening, remembering small details that others share, and of course, the handwritten letter. But Jimmy *does not send his team members a handwritten card*; instead, he sends *their loved ones* a card!

Can you imagine how your team member's spouse, mother, or significant other would react if they got a hand-addressed card from you?

In the card, Jimmy stated how much he appreciated them supporting his team member and for making them better. He let the loved one know that they, too, are also an important part of his team. He thanked them for enduring the hard work that he was sure their loved one carried home from time to time, and the long hours that occasionally interfered with family time.

I have done this for years and the inspiration it creates is nothing short of amazing. The significant others of our teams are usually on the outside looking in and have a very different perspective than the team members themselves. This rare and warm gesture often has a deep and lasting impact. The recipient is touched, but the team members are inspired because you care about the ones *they* care about.

BE ON A RELENTLESS MISSION TO INSPIRE!

If you want to build giants in the strongest way possible, you should not sometimes look for new ways that you can inspire your team; you should instead be on a relentless mission to inspire your team. But instead of racking your brain to come up with new and inventive ways to do so, just *be still* long enough to observe. Observation is an incredibly powerful leadership tool that is also overlooked because most everyone feels it should be a given; it is not. Being still, listening, and observing what others think and say are important. Emphasize those things. You must dedicate time, energy, and resources to this mission as it is the most important one.

"Not everything that can be counted, counts and not everything that counts can counted."—Albert Einstein

APPLICATION FOR INSPIRE EVERYONE

- As a leader, you have an obligation to inspire. You chose this role; this is your principal responsibility. The good news is, you get to figure out the best way to achieve this.
- Inspiration is different and deeper than motivation and must be purposeful and genuine to work.
- Slow down to speed up. Be still, listen, and notice what is important to your people.
- Create a big, scary, inspirational vision! Have conviction around a vision that scares you the first time you hear it and that inspires others to work toward a goal that is bigger than them.
- Trust the people you hire. If you don't trust them, fire them and hire people you do trust. Without trust, there can be no real team.
- Fear is the by-product of accountability. Fear occurs naturally and should not be purposefully instilled or used since that yields only short-term results and creates a poor culture.
- Stimulate the mind to inspire the heart. Ask great questions and talk about the things that are important to them!
- Inspiration is action. Take the initiative to do things that will inspire. Consider everything, as little things often count the most.
- Take time to invest in your people and to do little things that matter, like sending hand-written cards and notes—and not just to the team, but to others, as well.

GUT CHECK 14: Inspiring people is the full-time job of every leader, regardless of industry. People grow stronger and work harder, longer, and faster when they are inspired to do so. Inspiration leads to engagement, and an engaged team takes better care of clients and business. Will you be humble enough, and take the time required to be still long enough, to inspire everyone around you?

GIANT STEP THIRTEEN: STAY THE COURSE

Discipline determines victory

"Talent and potential without discipline turn into wasted opportunities." —Anonymous

Going to the gym one time will not make you fit, the same as reading one book will not make you smart. And you cannot become a great leader from doing something great one time. It is either a program or it's a fad: the choice is yours. You must be willing to believe in yourself and know that you have built a program that will best serve your team, clients, and company, and then execute the hell out of it! Once you have built your program, never get defensive, but rather remain open to criticism and suggestions. If things aren't going well, it will be up to you not to panic and react, and instead to make small corrections and be patient while those corrections are implemented. Don't second guess a solid program. Don't be scared to have high expectations. You aren't expecting too much—you may just be asking the wrong people, or asking at the wrong time.

The captain of a large ship once told me the following:

"Always chart your course well ahead of time because a large vessel will not turn on a dime. If you must change direction mid-course, make the corrections at the ship's wheel; but understand that the boat will only pitch slowly at first, and then begin to turn. At that point, you don't continue to make corrections; you give the boat a chance to respond to the corrections in the direction you've made. Overcorrecting could cause to you to damage the boat, cargo or crew, or disrupt the course entirely."

Build the program, make small corrections and have the discipline to **honor the program and stay the course**.

"Everyone must choose one of two pains: The pain of discipline or the pain of regret." —Jim Rohn

Building a successful program takes discipline, tenacity, and grit. It's not easy to stay the course and honor the program, especially because of the noise from the haters. Let me explain.

> *But first, a bit of math:*
> $6 \times 1 = 7$
> $6 \times 2 = 12$
> $6 \times 3 = 18$
> $6 \times 4 = 24$
> $6 \times 5 = 30$

If what you noticed first was that the first answer was wrong—congratulations! You are in the eightieth percentile of people in this world. The majority of people will first point out what is wrong.

Only around twenty percent will point out that eighty percent of my math was correct, or that I got the more difficult equations correct. As stated in the introduction, leaders must endure the 80/20 rule. In this instance, it means that people will *usually* only point out the twenty percent you did wrong, while never mentioning the eighty percent you are doing right. And for a leader, *usually* here means *always*.

When you look to bring the things you learned in this book to your own successful program, and implement things like the grandmother question, the 3Cs, or *better* practices, understand that people will ridicule you and your plans and ideas. They will tell you that it's dumb or just another thing that someone wrote. It is up to you to endure and do what you know is right and good for your people. Remember, *it is only dumb if it doesn't work.* **Stay the course; honor the program.**

DON'T SUCCUMB TO *THE LEADER KILLERS*

"The essence of strategy is choosing what not to do."
—*Michael Porter*

Bad leaders aren't necessarily dumb; they just succumb to what I call leader killers. We have all had bad leaders, and while some of them might be dumb, for the most part, I believe that poor leadership stems from four other attributes: **being an asshole, ego, pressure**, and **impatience**. I consider these to be leader killers because so many very smart and talented individuals go into to leadership positions and fail miserably because they let one or all of these traits into their life. Since the first one is addressed in Giant Step 2: Don't be an Asshole, let's focus on the other three here.

DON'T SUCCUMB TO THE *LEADER KILLERS*, PART 1: CHECK YOUR EGO AT THE DOOR

You must keep ego in check and the best way to do that is to *serve*.

"The hardest part about serving others for most people, is they see it as a weakness, when it is really the ultimate act of strength."

— *Mikeal R. Morgan*

It takes a strong person to selflessly serve others and it is in this act alone that one can be considered a leader without ever having the title. Ask yourself this question about everything you do in a day: How do your actions serve others? When the answer is consistently, *"They don't, they only serve me,"* CHANGE. At this point, you are succumbing to ego and need to check yourself. Great leaders aren't egomaniacal narcissists, because to be great, you must be authentic and if that is the real you, no one will ever follow you long-term. When in doubt, serve. If it feels weird, serve more. This is because if you can't let ego go, your best bet is to not hold leadership positions until you can get your ego in check.

The other part of letting go of ego is giving credit when and where it is due. So many team members I've talked to through the years tell me story after story of how their leader took credit for their work. Remember, you work for the team, not the other way around, so all work is their work. If you are looking for recognition, get back on the front line. Leaders should seek recognition *for* their team, not *from* their team. Most great leaders would prefer to give credit to the team for something they didn't do, versus take credit for something they did. **Stay the course; honor the program.**

DON'T SUCCUMB TO THE *LEADER KILLERS*, PART 2:
NO PRESSURE, NO DIAMONDS

The issue of pressure is significantly more complex and difficult to use properly. Pressure can be used for good; after all, it is what turns ordinary coal into a diamond. Pressure is everywhere in leadership and can also be a bad thing. Just as when a child is pressured by peers to be foolish, foolish things usually happen, and pressure in leadership can be similar. Pressure can heighten a sense of urgency, generate excitement, and push people in good ways. But too much pressure or pressure applied incorrectly can be devastating. I have collected so many examples of a leader who creates, outlines, communicates, and executes a great plan, yet still fails miserably. How can that be?

In a word, pressure. Leadership is about doing what is right, not what is easy. The bottom line is, a great leadership plan is like a great foundation for a building. It is considerably more expensive and takes longer to create, typically because is it deeper and made with care and not haste. And like a properly laid, great foundation, a great leadership plan will stand the test of time and will be stable to build on, and while not always first to come up, will be the last to go down. This is too much for some people to understand and so when pressure is introduced, even leaders who know that they should stay the course, honor the program and build the best foundation, too often succumb.

If the process gets rushed, people get pressed, and everything falls apart. Much like an electrical insulator is used in electrical equipment to separate electrical conductors without allowing current through, in these situations, great leaders will act as pressure insulators, preventing the bad pressure from passing to the team.

What about pressure on the team itself? We have all used pressure to push ourselves or others in one way or another to be great or to achieve some positive result. It is simply the lack of balance in applying pressure that turns it from diamond maker to dust maker. A lump of coal will only turn into a diamond if the pressure, conditions, foundation and timing are perfect! As a leader, you must take on the seemingly impossible task of balancing the pressure that is applied to your team. Stay focused and pay close attention to the small verbal and nonverbal clues out there. Keep in mind that you must be close to your people to hear and see these whispers. Listen so that you can tell when the pressure is too much or is applied incorrectly. When you can balance pressure and use it for good, you can exponentially increase results and have people at peak production without burning out. **Stay the course; honor the program.**

DON'T SUCCUMB TO THE *LEADER KILLERS,* PART 3: GROWTH AND DEVELOPMENT TAKE TIME

Seeds planted in a garden today are not ready for harvest tomorrow. The seeds must be cared for, provided with light, hydration, and nutrients, as well as the appropriate climate and environment. There is also a considerable amount of patience involved. The same is true with the growth and development of people.

A proper business program should be set up similarly to how a farmer sets up fields for planting by ensuring that all elements for proper growth are present. Once you have all the elements and execute the plan, you, too, must exercise patience and let the seeds grow.

Keep in mind that growth takes time. Don't second guess the plan because you do not see growth right away. Only start re-evaluating the program if your results go in the wrong direction.

I call lack of patience a leader killer because I have seen so many leaders fail because they insist on rushing growth. There is nothing wrong with a *balance* of pressure and urgency, as long as you include patience in the equation. Challenge yourself to learn to love the process. By doing so, you will not only understand but appreciate what goes into building giants. **Stay the course; honor the program.**

KEEP AN EVEN AND BALANCED APPROACH.

"You're never as good as everyone tells you when you win, and you're never as bad as they say when you lose." —Lou Holtz

Never let your emotions get too high or too low when leading people. You are going to feel on top of the world some days, and you are going to have those days when nothing goes right. Great leaders understand balance and that everything they do or say has a consequence. You cannot take back the things you say in a heated moment, and you can't successfully lead a team when you're sad, with your head down in your hands.

You can get a better handle on this by contemplating for a few extra minutes how you feel about a situation, and how you *should* feel about it if you take the emotion out of it. You also should consider the long-term impact of each decision you make. Ask yourself how this decision will impact people, business, and markets in the future. Don't react just because something is really good or really bad right now, and cause a negative future impact; instead, consider how the decision—and even how you feel about the situation—will impact all aspects of the future. If the situation won't matter much in a few months or years, don't stay upset for very long right now. Learn to let go of the bullshit and hold onto what matters. Learn to value progress. **Stay the course; honor the program.**

MEASURE THE PROGRESS OF THE PROGRAM, NOT ONE OR TWO INDIVIDUALS.

A great leadership program is one where progress is made by the team and not just one or two individuals. When you examine teams that consistently win, even in sports like football, you find that while all winning teams have star players, they win consistently because of the strength of the whole program. A program that reinforces things like every person doing *their job* well, not making stupid mistakes by having too many men on the field, or offside penalties, and not turning the football over, are programs that ultimately win championships. Some people ridicule coaches for spending inordinate amounts of time practicing the most basic drills that strengthen these skills, but these coaches know that they are looking for progress and even if things go poorly at first, the program will not be destroyed over one or two losses because they know progress is being made. These leaders understand that individual star players come and go, but the championship is always within reach because of the strength of the program. World-famous, American football coach Vince Lombardi told his team of professional football players in a well-known speech that, "this is a football."

Most in his audience had played the game since they could walk, yet here he was explaining what a football was. He also took the time to walk the men onto the field and would show each of them the location of the out-of-bounds markers, yard lines, end-zones, and goal posts. He explained in great detail the basic rules of the game and each player's roles and responsibilities. These seemed like table stakes, yet Coach Lombardi spent the time, energy, and focus on basics because he knew that if his team could execute the fundamentals, their skills and determination would be effective and even multiplied. **Stay the course; honor the program.**

FOCUS YOUR 80 ON THE 20

The 80/20 theory explained by Richard Koch, author of *The Secret to Achieving More with Less*, is that *"eighty percent of products, or customers or employees, are only contributing twenty percent of profits; that there is great waste; that the most powerful resources of the company are being held back by a majority of much less effective resources; that profits could be multiplied if more of the best sort of products could be sold, employees hired, or customers attracted (or convinced to buy more from the firm)."*

Ninety percent of the leaders surveyed for this book agreed and said that, because they believe this theory to be true, leaders should focus eighty percent of their time, energy, and effort on the top twenty percent. The rest shouldn't be neglected, but the focus should be on making the top twenty percent of performers better, happier, and even more productive. **Stay the course; honor the program.**

WHEN CAN I CALL MYSELF A GIANT BUILDER?

The trick is to never know! Great leaders never truly believe that they are great enough and therefore never stop trying to achieve this status. Remember that even when others refer to you as a great leader—while it's nice to hear—these are only words, and actions always speak louder than words.

1. Have you created followers or other leaders?
2. Have you consistently inspired, influenced, and made people better, smarter, or happier?
3. Will people willingly follow you anywhere?
4. Does your team succeed if you are not around?
5. Will people stay even when the going gets tough?
6. Would people follow you if you left?
7. Are you a role model, even during times of complete chaos?
8. Are people positively impacted by you and your message? How?
9. Can you stimulate people to think and inspire them to act?
10. Can you see further because you are standing on the shoulders of the giants that you built?

CONSIDER YOUR LEADERSHIP LEGACY

Consider how you want to be remembered by the world as more than just a brand or for one thing or another. What legacy are you leaving? And how do you ensure that you are positively contributing to that legacy each day?

I often ask people if they would act differently if they were followed by a film crew that publicly aired their every move. As leaders, we are in that level of spotlight, every second of every day.

Every company, every project, and every single interaction you have each day is examined (and aired) by someone. Good or bad, people are impacted by you and your message more significantly than you may think, and that is why it is critical that you make sure everything you do adds as much value as possible. Leave a leadership legacy that you will be proud of and remember that everything you do each day is a part of that legacy. Don't be a leader for the eighty percent of people who will be inevitably be your harshest critics; do it for the twenty percent who want to win and are willing to work like hell for it. Do it for the giants.

Thank you for investing in yourself by taking these giant steps with me. I would like to close by asking you to always selflessly serve others and put people first. Love and develop your team. Do your very best to simplify everything you touch and relentlessly inspire everyone around you. Invest in culture, and your people will invest in your business. Honor the program and maintain disciplined execution. Always be the most authentic version of yourself and give this world and its people everything you've got!

"When I stand before God at the end of my life, I would hope that I would not have a single bit of talent left. And I could say, 'I used everything you gave me.'" —Erma Bombeck

FINAL GUT CHECK: Will you endure the hard times without panic so that you can carry out the mission with compassion and conviction? Will you make small course corrections and honor the program, as you expect others to? Will you be a committed leader who has a keen EQ, puts people first, simplifies everything, and inspires everyone? To lead is to serve, so, "if serving is beneath you, leadership is beyond you!" -Anonymous.

"Whoever wants to be great among you will be your servant. Whoever wants to be first among you will be your slave. Just as Jesus didn't come to be served, but rather to serve and to give his life to liberate many people." —Matthew 20:26-28, The Holy Bible

MORE INFORMATION

About the Author

Mikeal R. Morgan learned valuable lessons as he endured a youth riddled with poverty, poor health, violence, and a lack of education. For decades, he has successfully combined life's hard lessons with business acumen and a love of serving people in order to rise through the ranks of business and to become a proven leader, sought-after speaker, and celebrated author. For years, Mikeal has successfully led teams in multiple industries, and specializes in rebuilding and leading underperforming teams from change and uncertainty to excellence.

Mikeal's work is proven to sustain growth, development, and award-winning performance. Simple to understand, and easy to implement, Mikeal's strategies transform people into performers.

Mikeal is a husband, father of five, and President of Phoenix Training Innovations, a company dedicated to helping people and companies look better, feel better, and make more money. Mikeal's powerful messages move people to meaningful action because the audience is as inspired as they are informed. Passionate, driven, and committed, Mikeal is boldly leading a life of faith, purpose, and love so that he leaves a legacy of value.

Let Mikeal help you build leaders who build giants!

Mikeal specializes in, and is available for, the following:

- Inspirational keynote speeches
- Consulting on leadership, process efficiencies, technology, simplification, policy, sales and marketing strategies, safety, and more
- Multi-day, custom training programs for leadership, sales, prospecting, and more
- Helping you hire for important positions within your organization
- Hosting brainstorm sessions
- Introducing *How to Build Giants* to your organization with a live, interactive training program that highlights the key principles from this book—an investment with a tremendous and immediate return on investment

Please contact Mikeal at www.mikealmorgan.com to learn more.

Made in the USA
Middletown, DE
30 January 2020